BEYOND BULLSH*T

BEYOND BULLSH*T

Straight-Talk at Work

Samuel A. Culbert

STANFORD BUSINESS BOOKS
An Imprint of Stanford University Press
Stanford, California

Stanford University Press
Stanford, California

Printed in the United States of America on acid-free, archival-quality paper

Library of Congress Cataloging-in-Publication Data

Culbert, Samuel A.
  Beyond bullsh*t : straight-talk at work / Samuel A. Culbert.
    p. cm.
  Includes bibliographical references and index.
  ISBN 978-0-8047-5885-7 (cloth : alk. paper)
  1. Business communication. 2. Communication in management. 3.
Corporate culture. 4. Organizational behavior. 5. Interpersonal relations.
I. Title. II. Title: Beyond bullsh*t.

HF5718.C84 2008
658.4'5—dc22

                                2007029377

Designed by Bruce Lundquist
Typeset at Stanford University Press in 10.75/17 Sabon

Rosella

CONTENTS

FOREWORD
*Palimpsest**

Every secret of a writer's soul, every experience of his life,
every quality of his mind is written large in his works.
Virginia Woolf

VIRGINIA WOOLF'S QUOTE could have been written expressly for Sam Culbert. As you'll see in his Prologue, this is the book Culbert has been writing about, teaching about, and consulting about throughout his distinguished career. And it all began since he was an observant, wide-eyed 10-year-old, growing up in a big, expansive city in an airless, quarantined family. To quote Woolf again, "Nothing has really happened until it's recorded." In this remarkable, groundbreaking book, Sam has finally recorded his ruminations and wonders about those persistent demons that block our everyday, and often futile, attempts to establish direct, valid, candid human relationships. This is what Culbert and his book is all about: Bringing people in, not shutting them out. Scraping away those interpersonal scrims that fog up the windows of human transparency. Creating the gorgeous space of mutual discovery of reality. The pleasure of really, yes really, *knowing* the others we often haplessly miss or mistake or pass by in everyday life.

---

* A manuscript, usually written in papyrus, on which more than one text has been written with the earlier writing incompletely erased and still visible.

This isn't the author's first time at bat, so to speak, about these human scrabbles. It's been his signature *leitmotif* for the last forty or so years. It's just that this book is more emboldened and written with telling examples and representative anecdotes that not only enliven his framework but give the reader—at least this one—a *déjà vu* feeling. Yes, I've been there. How could I have screwed up that interpersonal exchange. "Omigod," as my students might exclaim, "How could I have done such a ridiculous thing!?" All that and more.

Reading *Beyond Bullsh*t* reminds me a little of reading Erving Goffman's classic, *The Presentation of Self in Everyday Life*, about fifty years ago. It jolted me into an alarming awareness of my inauthentic "faces" I put on for the other. It made it possible for me to translate the present into something I could understand, even change. It was a reality, new to me, even a bother to me, that crucially helped me to translate the present reality. This book, Culbert's master stroke, has the power to transform the nature of how we relate to one another, freshly imagine each other and nourish our lives with others. *Beyond Bullsh*t* will become a classic in its own right.

I love this book and the courage to put it out there, which for some, maybe an unwelcome mirror to one's way of viewing reality. I'm reminded of a quote from Ray Bradbury's *Fahrenheit 451*:

We need not be alone. We need to be really bothered once in awhile. How long has it been since you were really bothered? About something important, about something real?

Sam is a supreme "botherer," about something important and real.

Warren Bennis   Santa Monica, CA

PROLOGUE

I LEARNED ABOUT BULLSH*T and acquired a desire for straight-talk the same way most people do: as a child growing up in a family where what people said they were doing and the reasons they gave failed to match-up with what I saw taking place. In my family the disparities were extreme and this turned out to be an advantage. Had they occurred less often or been more subtle I might have been taken in. Early on I sensed deception and I struggled to talk explicitly about what was plainly apparent to me.

I derived comfort thinking my parents were unaware of the duplicity and their unwillingness to speak candidly about our lives. Pushing them to do so made me the family irritant. My much older sister was no help; she accepted and practiced the family's go-along-to-get-along ways. As a result, I alone was held to blame for family discord. The family's unspoken message: if only I would knuckle under, accept what I was told, and control myself, there would be calm. School was no better. The teachers' typical reaction to my mother being called in to discuss my deportment was, "How could a boy like you have such a lovely mother?"

My mother suffered depressive episodes that apparently began with my birth. No one ever talked about her paralyzing lows or called attention to those terrifying occasions when her spirit seemed to be absent. Through Christian Science she developed an ability to appear upbeat even when she was down. She observed surface protocol and outwardly gave what was socially expected. The times she was authentically present were treasured moments for me. Then I experienced support and felt loved. But I wanted to talk about the abandonment I felt when her persona was mostly pretense, when I found myself alone without love, guidance, or protection. On the other hand, her down episodes forced me to develop a great deal of independence. Out of necessity I learned early on to fend for myself.

My father was a heavy evening drinker and strong-willed disciplinarian. I rebelled against his attempts to control me whenever I could. Fortunately he often fell asleep just as family conflicts were heating up. Ironically his drinking was my best defense. His half-drunk attempts to "rein Sam in for his own good" were so obviously outrageous that most punishments were rescinded. My need to talk straight in the midst of all this pretense couldn't be stifled. For bolstering I sought support and "reality checks" from others, often people from outside my immediate family. I found outsiders were often able to grasp what insiders couldn't see. In the process, I developed a distrust of authority, a questioning attitude about anything for which I couldn't see the basis, and the ability to read behavioral clues that might help predict what was coming next.

My mother's condition gave me unusual freedom. I would leave the house in the morning and return just before dinner. By the age of 10 I had access to anywhere I wanted to go in Chicago.

My father was a middle-income earner and my mother made sure I always had carfare, allowing me to hop a bus, a street car, or the El at my whim. I could go almost anywhere—crosstown movies, a park to play ball, downtown to see the eye doctor, Evanston to buy stamps for my collection, and, with increasing frequency, to Wrigley Field. Being a die-hard Cubs fan partially accounts for my intrepid, dogged optimism. I tend to view adversity and setbacks as veiled opportunities. You'd be amazed how much stuff I've sorted through looking for the pony.

In those days even children could get permits to work in the summer. Turning 12 I got a "plum job" in my uncle's asbestos factory. It paid 85 cents an hour with time and a half for overtime. Reaching the factory required taking a bus to the elevated train and then walking half a mile through an African American neighborhood where neighbors routinely sat talking on their porches and stoops and children played games in the streets. This was prior to affordable air conditioning so, in the summer, the streets bustled with people seeking refuge from the sweltering indoor heat. This exotic-seeming neighborhood was the antithesis of my silent, cloistered one, and every aspect of it fascinated and instructed me.

At work I was fortunate to be guided and protected by a wise and generous "Negro" foreman. He was the first authority I felt I could trust. Watching Tim Matthews I learned the benefits of picking your moments and how to avoid being labeled "the troublemaker." He showed me how to sidestep harsh treatment by the factory boss, a war-damaged refugee who referred to himself as "The Big Litvak." Precious were the invitations to accompany Tim, along with his wife, three young children, and extended family on picnic outings. Tragically, Tim died an early and ugly asbestos-related death. But to this day I have poignant memories of what I learned from time spent with him and his family.

Cut to the present. I have a bachelor's degree in systems engineering, a Ph.D. in clinical psychology, and a career spent exposing and demystifying the bullsh*t far too common in corporations and other organizations. Looking back on my youth, I wonder if I have spent most of my life working out my childhood dilemma. Now, as then, I have a need to talk straight about what most people are too willing to ignore.

I've now spent almost forty years as a university-based researcher and professor with the world of work as my laboratory. Part-time consulting engagements have given me ready access to phenomena I choose to study—and "carfare" for doing so. My purpose has long been to expose bullsh*t and misguided behavior in the workplace and then, using what I have learned, to show others—students, managers, and readers—how they might be more effective, both personally and professionally. This book is a natural successor to my last one, *Don't Kill the Bosses!*,[1] which told how to recognize and avoid the pitfalls of boss-dominated relationships. That volume followed naturally from my *Mind-Set Management*,[2] which probed the little understood role that each individual's personal life history plays in every aspect of corporate life.

My own journey has taught me a great deal about what people need to live and work more effectively, including how to function successfully as part of a team. What I've learned has taught me to ask myriad questions of the people I want to know. I probe to understand what's important to them so I can react appropriately in light of what their words and actions *really* mean. If I have a creed, it is that no one is exactly like me and that everyone is different from everyone else. This is in stark contrast to an assumption that many people make: that everyone else thinks just as they do or, even worse, should think just as they do. In my experience those people make lousy managers and bosses.

In the course of cutting through mountains of bullsh*t and pretense, I've learned to recognize those occasions when straight-talk is neither possible nor desirable. I have come to respect the truth that people sometimes need the façades they so artfully construct. And I have come to appreciate the WD-40 function some institutional bullsh*t plays, keeping dissatisfaction from escalating and maintaining enough civility that painful differences can sometimes be worked out. A case in point: the * (asterisk) in my use of the word "bullsh*t." Many readers will see this as pretense and think "how can I believe a guy who writes about bullsh*t and won't even spell out the word?" Be assured that I am fully aware of the compromise I made. I mulled the alternatives for months. In the end, I decided the somewhat coy usage was the best way to ensure readership among those people who need that * in order to seek what might be useful to them in this book.

This book is full of short anecdotes that illustrate its main points. Each and every one is rooted in events I have personally experienced. In the course of my ongoing research, I encounter new examples every day. Of course I know you encounter them as well. You may even think you know some of the people I've described. To avoid embarrassing individuals who have done the best they could and would like to learn from their mistakes, I've changed names and camouflaged locations. Sometimes you have to protect the guilty. What's more, I like when their lawyers stay away. Now to the book.

INTRODUCTION

1 GETTING STRAIGHT-TALK AT WORK

He was a "dead man walking." After only four months on the job the decision to replace the new vice president of marketing had been made. A mismanaged photo shoot and botched seasonal promotion left his bosses convinced he lacked judgment and essential skills. They began looking through him when he spoke.

The bosses wanted him out immediately but decided to wait three weeks until people he recruited were settled in and productive. Important work needed to be done. Although the vice president thought he was still on his corporate honeymoon, he was actually on executive death row.

In the view of the bosses, the VP's only accomplishment was attracting three new managers with promise, each in the process of joining the firm. One was a proven marketer making a crosstown move for a better title and more pay. A second planned to begin as soon as her teenage son was settled in his new school. The third was flying in Thursday to meet new associates prior to finalizing his deal. This would be his second post-MBA assignment. He saw it as career-building important and was asking all the right questions. Prominent in his thinking was mentoring by this "very savvy" VP and getting in on the ground floor of the elite marketing group being built.

Only a few insiders had been told, but others with keen eyes had figured out what the VP had not. The guy waiting for the coffin is always the last to connect the dots. Years of observing the dynamics of corporate success and covering backsides teach astute employees to recognize when someone is being treated as a ghost.

The looming termination complicated life for all involved. Those in the know or just suspecting dealt with marketing topics with superficial politeness but no real enthusiasm. What else is there to do when you know that whatever's decided is likely to be undone? To avoid wasting time those in the know surfed marketing department e-mails, deleting most without responding. Knowledgeable bosses substituted underlings to represent them in marketing-topic meetings but provided little in the way of briefing. When subordinates asked for more information, they were merely told that their participation would be good training. They quickly got the message—"look plausible, ask questions, but don't commit to anything." Their job was to look relevant discussing topics that were not.

To the surprise of clued-in executives, interacting with the newly recruited managers turned out to be far more challenging than dealing with the about-to-exit VP. The bosses would need their trust and respect after the VP departed. But what do you say to a young person sharing his excitement about working with an executive whom you have decided is incompetent and should be fired? How do you establish trust while perpetuating an illusion? How do you earn respect from subordinates you are asking to participate in time-wasting meetings? How do you maintain self-respect when sending sham messages to a well-meaning executive being buried in an avalanche of inauthentic behavior? And what do you say to everyone else who, after the coffin is shut, will think you deliberately misled them? While this situation is unique, there's little unique about the challenges involved. In one form or another, it's what people face every day at work.

THIS BOOK is for people who wonder what it's going to take to get rid of the constant deception and obfuscation that, at the end of the work day, leaves them feeling beaten up, confused, and even a little dirty. It is also for people greeting them at home wondering "What's going on there that takes such a toll?" Pressed for an answer, many explain "it's all that bullsh*t I had to endure." They blame abstractions such as "the system," "the incompetence around me," "too much bureaucracy"—at a loss to pinpoint a precise cause. Even people who disdain deception find themselves involved. They too speak bullsh*t at work.

Being misled and misleading others is part of the daily routine. It flows naturally, just as we saw in the opening saga of the doomed vice president of marketing. Expecting this, people become disheartened. Few can envision finding a job where they can relax and straightforwardly say what they think. People instinctively hunger for a culture of straight-talk, even as they are hard-pressed to say what would make "all that bullsh*t" go away. I'm not just talking about other people. It's a scourge that affects us all.

Straight-talk at work! There isn't much we crave more yet get less of. We want others to say candidly what they think, be forthcoming about what they have done, and be up front about what they are planning. We want honest reactions to what we propose; we want to believe our views are receiving serious consideration; we want to know when others are no longer listening with open minds; we want to hear the real reason someone resists doing what we have asked—we want to know where we stand. Instead, what we mostly get is bullsh*t—in spoken words and in actions taken. Worst of all, the bullsh*t sometimes comes so disguised we don't even recognize it as such.

There are, though, special moments when others tell it to us straight—even when their views differ from ours. They refrain from euphemism, don't spin their words, forthrightly relate all relevant facts, share their feelings, and may even go so far as to reveal what they personally have at stake. In other words, there are times—albeit rare ones—when others tell us the naked truth as they know it. We love it when others don't obscure what they mean, mislead us, or lull us into thinking their agendas include our interests unless they actually do. These are moments to treasure.

Decades of research and consulting with professionals and managers have convinced me that straight-talk at work *is* possible. But it *requires* more than luck and willing people. Straight-talk is the product of thoughtful, caring relationships built on trust by people committed to looking out for one another's success. It entails much more than let-the-chips-fall-where-they-may candor and blunt start-to-finish honesty. And, it's not brought about by cat-and-mouse, testing-the-waters conversation that evolves into a tell-it-straight, see if you can get the other person to reciprocate discussion. *Straight-talk* is a caring, other-sensitive, candor-on-demand, loyalty-producing, intimacy-escalating, give-and-take relationship leading to enhanced personal and organizational productivity.

Compounding the difficulties of getting *straight-talk* at work is the ever-present need to pretend that "straight-talk" is already taking place. We know it isn't but the rules of the corporate-speak force us to behave as if it were ubiquitous. Everyone needs others to think they're telling "it" perfectly straight. No one ever begins a conversation by saying, "Listen carefully while I bullsh*t you." People strike a sincere pose, look you squarely in the eyes, and then deliver a stream of self-serving verbiage designed to get your support for their agendas. It's business as usual.

Usually what we're getting is so obvious there's little need to allege deception. It's corporately correct advocacy carefully composed to appear logical, rational, and objective. Our role is to look friendly, nod appropriately, and, when possible, feign sufficient agreement to get away with asking the questions that allow us to decide the impact a proposal is likely to have on us. If we conclude what's advocated is not sufficiently self-advantageous, we push back, citing the proposal's failure to serve the organization, never its failure to benefit us. In other words, we block other people's bullsh*t with some of our own.

Everyone knows that succeeding at work requires us to spin what we say, withhold some of what we know, and pretend to believe things that we know to be untrue. At work we're constantly challenged to trust what others tell us. But at the end of the day, we know that all communications are designed, first and foremost, to advance the self-interested agendas of the communicators. That may sound cynical, but it is also true. Like every other aspect of life, the world at work is driven by self-interests. Straight-talk begins by facing up to the fact that ours is a self-interested world.

No question about it. Getting straight-talk at work is often an arduous task, requiring skill, sensitivity, and judgment. When a person wanting straight-talk doesn't see us reciprocating, even when our intention is to tell it straight, we can count on the conversation going south. We all know the drill and inevitable outcome. Bullsh*t perceived leads to bullsh*t dispensed.

On the other hand, straight-talk met with straight-talk has the potential to create invaluable bonds, even when our viewpoint doesn't prevail. How can we win when we lose? Because straight-talk reveals the other person's self-interests, and such a revelation can produce understanding and respect, no matter whose position prevails. Sensing our respect, others become friendlier and more accommodating, eager to "purchase" additional good will and support. It's a fact that being known as a straight-talker is a form of interpersonal currency today.

Taken from an organizational perspective, there's no greater contribution to operational effectiveness and success than conversations in which people with conflicting viewpoints discuss their differences forthrightly. In fact, decades of researching how managers function have convinced me that straight-talk leading to trusting relationships is the quintessential management tool.[1] With straight-talk, mistakes in planning and action can be quickly rectified, and people—even those with marked limitations—are able to lead more effectively. With straight-talk, missteps can be studied and corrected without blame being laid or inadequacy implied, saving all the energy typically squandered on those pointless activities.

Without straight-talk even the best-laid plans and most expertly executed actions often fail to have the desired effects. Instead, groups splinter and individuals become jurisdictional, image conscious, self-protective, and competitive with their teammates; they hide their mistakes, fail to self-correct, persist in dissembling—the list is endless. From the organization's standpoint, straight-talk and the trusting relationships it creates is an invaluable asset that ought to be listed on the year-end financial statement under "Corporate Assets and Accumulated Goodwill."

But too often, bullsh*t is the elephant in the room that blocks people from talking straight. And it's an elephant rarely dealt with until its presence becomes too blatant to ignore. At that point, someone may finally sneeze out *"bullsh*t."* However, sneezing out "bullsh*t" is seldom enough to nullify its negative impacts. Much more is required to deal with it effectively, beginning with distinguishing it from truth-telling, from candor, and from straight-talk.

Until you can recognize the bullsh*t in the "truths" people tell you and understand why they resort to it, often unconsciously, you're ill prepared to decide whether straight-talk is even possible. Thus the first step in getting more straight-talk is better understanding of what bullsh*t is and why even the best-intentioned people use it as an ever-ready, essential personal tool. You need to know what its use accomplishes. Bullsh*t persists in organizational life because it works, and we can't get beyond it until we understand why it's so often necessary.

A deeper understanding of bullsh*t and more skill at spotting it can make a critical difference in your effectiveness. Doing so will require your finding ways to demystify workplace communications, to interpret the complex messages your colleagues send, whatever their claims to candor. Shortly I'll explain why bullsh*t has become the *etiquette of choice* in corporate communications. Understanding that will help you initiate a more rewarding alternative—straight-talk. This is covered in Chapters 2–4.

> Bullsh*t has become the etiquette of choice in corporate communications.

My goal in writing this book is to help you get more straight-talk into your work life. At a minimum, the book should make it easier for you to spot bullsh*t and avoid many of its negative consequences. It contains perspective and advice that should enhance your ability to turn pedestrian conversations into straight-talk, even when you and the people with whom you are interacting don't think candor is possible. This is the subject of Chapters 5–7.

No doubt experience has already taught you that straight-talk is seldom easy and there are times when it would prove to be a liability. One of my aims is to help you recognize situations in which straight-talk is not in your best interest and should not be attempted. But I would also like to give you some tools you can use to put more straight-talk into your organizational life, for both the company's and your benefit.

Developing straight-talk relationships requires self-and other-sensitivity skills that you probably already have but are not yet fully applying. There are many times when you and your colleagues would prefer straight-talk, if only you knew how to make it happen. This book should help you achieve that goal, whether you are the initiator of a conversation or the recipient. This is the subject of Chapters 8–11.

Many obstacles to straight-talk will be presented in hope you can avoid them. While the concept of straight-talk sounds simple, achieving it is complex. It is impossible to do so in a relationship steeped in distrust. For that reason it is often easier to put the principles of straight-talk to work in new relationships, before suspicions and conflicts have emerged. Those principles provide a mechanism for converting the human desire to cooperate and bond in the pursuit of common goals by building trusting relationships that endure. You'll find some nuanced guidance for doing this in Chapter 12.

While the book addresses the world of work, it could just as easily have been written about other areas of life. I've only come across a few books that seriously address the topic of bullsh*t and I cite them below.[2] In contrast to the others, this book acknowledges that there are times when bullsh*t is necessary to team effectiveness and times when bullsh*t impedes it. In every instance it's a determination you'll have to make. My hope is that reading these pages will help you in building honest relationships that lead to enhanced effectiveness at work and everywhere else.

I've never written a book that goes "Step 1, Step 2, this is how you do it." I believe that such how-to guides inevitably oversimplify their subject and also require the author to know much more than I know about you and the real-life situations you encounter and create. At the end of the day, I believe each of us is self-invented. In these pages, I hope you will find insights, skills, and information that you can tap each day as you respond to a steady stream of people who can never tell you more of the truth that they know.

I-speak is one of the techniques I recommend that is key to forming straight-talk relationships. I hope you will learn how to initiate straight-talk, even with your boss, and when it is best avoided. Later in the book, I will introduce you to what I call truth-finding. This is a critically important process for demystifying and interpreting the words and behavior of others. Chapter 11 presents some methods for determining the meaning of behavior you don't quite understand. Among the simple but powerful techniques is asking yourself "Why this now?" as a way of determining the intentions of others before responding to their words and actions. I also recommend the use of "active questioning" to gain insight into the motivations of others. Taken together, these techniques should enhance your ability to understand the other person's truth, making it far easier for you to respond appropriately. These are tools that you may find yourself using in all your important relationships from now on. Mostly I will give you a context for evaluating and responding to others, with a few prescriptions along the way. It's up to you to construct your own plan for deciphering and responding to the messages that others send.

Finally, a word of warning. Like it or not, you're going to have to make peace with an unpleasant fact. The vast majority of work-life interactions require that you *not* call people on their bullsh*t. Why? Because, as I am about to explain, bullsh*t often serves important workplace functions. The open-ended question you're going to have to ask is "When is it possible to move beyond bullsh*t?" to reap the many benefits straight-talk at work can offer.

THEORY SECTION — BULLSH*T

2

BULLSH*T

Is It the Nemesis?

It was entirely predictable that the issue of executive compensation would be raised at Home Depot's 2006 shareholder's meeting. Independent analysts had calculated the CEO's five-year compensation package to be nearly a quarter of a billion dollars during a period when the stock had declined 17 percent. But when the compensation question was raised, CEO Bob Nardelli categorically dismissed it on grounds it wasn't on the posted agenda. Looking for another director for an appeal was fruitless. Nardelli was the only director in the room and he clearly didn't speak for outside shareholders. Asked about the absence of other directors, Nardelli responded that each was at headquarters attending to corporate business. Angered by Nardelli's arrogance, someone shouted "bullsh*t!"

Even with nine shareholder proposals on the docket, the entire agenda was dispatched in just 30 minutes. A few days later, the webcast of those 30 minutes disappeared from the homedepot .com web page. About the same time, Home Depot issued a press release stating that all directors would attend next year's meeting. However, Nardelli will not be among them, since he *was forced to resign in January 2007, as much for his arrogance as for his outsized pay-for-non-performance package. Nardelli left with a golden parachute worth another $210 million—the ultimate bullsh*t in the minds of angry shareholders.*

UNDERSTANDING HOW to get more straight-talk at work requires an examination of what many call its nemesis, *bullsh*t*. If you're one of the many, you probably don't realize the essential and surprisingly constructive roles bullsh*t plays. Many times the authenticity of relationships and veracity of spoken content gets subordinated to mere cosmetics at work. Under those circumstances bullsh*t becomes the salve that eases myriad frictions. It's surprising but true: bullsh*t is essential for workplace harmony.

The recent best-seller essay, *On Bullshit*, written by Princeton University philosopher Harry Frankfurt, did much to deepen my understanding of bullsh*t. It did so by distinguishing *bullsh*t* from *lying* and other deceptions that baffle and disorient us at work. Frankfurt explains that lying requires a communicator to think about the truth, as he or she knows it, and then to consciously decide to portray some matter differently than he or she actually believes to be case. Thus, as Frankfurt explains, telling a lie requires that the perpetrator first reflect on what he or she thinks is true. That makes it intentional, premeditated deception.

You can extend what Frankfurt says about verbal behavior to physical actions. Then any conscious action that leads someone to do what they would not normally choose to do should also be considered a lie. Such acts may be relatively subtle forms of deception on the perpetrator's part, such as giving someone an assignment that sets them up to fail or giving them a nominal promotion without enhancements in pay, jurisdiction, or function. Of course, lying also includes blatantly fraudulent acts such as cheating, reneging on promises, and slander.

In contrast, Frankfurt sees bullshit driven by what is expedient in the moment, without the communicator considering whether the words or actions represent truth, non-truth, corporate pretense, "literary license," or flat-out deception. With bullsh*t, the communicator's goal is persuasion, not veracity or double-dealing. Any deception that takes place is merely the inadvertent consequence of the communicator's working their agenda of the moment. With bullsh*t, the communicator's mind is focused exclusively on framing his or her appeal persuasively. There is little, if any, concern or conscience for whether the communicator's words, acts, and emotional appeals correspond to the truth as that person knows it. The focus is all but exclusively on what needs to be said to get the other person's concurrence.

In bullsh*t mode, any concern for the factual is prompted solely by the communicator's desire for credibility. The communicator's compass isn't pointed at the truth. His or her sole purpose is to mount a compelling appeal for a self-serving agenda, whether or not cited facts are true is incidental. The communicator's only concern is maintaining plausibility for what's alleged in the appeal. The opening anecdote describes Bob Nardelli pushing the process past its limits. Shareholders might have continued to pretend all was well at Home Depot if he had maintained the illusion that he cared about their input. Instead of trying to persuade, he steamrolled and shareholders rebelled. After all, to be effective, even bullsh*t requires some finesse.

Most serious essays on bullsh*t focus on communications on explicit topics.[1] The parties know what issues are being discussed. In such instances recipients of bullsh*t have the opportunity to question, either aloud or in their own minds, the veracity, comprehensiveness, relevance, and personal consequences of the communicator's words and actions. Whether or not they make the effort to conduct the research depends on whether they see a benefit for themselves.

It's debatable whether people who go along with an appeal they view as bullsh*t, no matter how much they nod their heads, feign agreement, and pretend the communication is factually credible, rise to *bullsh*t-initiating* status. Clearly, received bullsh*t becomes bullsh*t initiated when someone repeats a story that they believe is bullsh*t to a third party, perhaps trying to play it both ways. Beginning a conversation with "You know what I heard," or "Here's what Jon Kovak told me" allows them to duck authorship and to avoid accountability for the truthfulness of a message. In such cases, bullsh*t *in* and repackaged qualifies as bullsh*t *out*. Moreover, tacit acceptance and feigned endorsement—giving the impression that a bullsh*t message received is valid while thinking differently—is at least bullsh*t and maybe a lie. Why? Because the agenda served by pretending the message is valid is relationship harmony. The bullsh*t recipient is now sending their own message—a willingness to pretend the communicator's message is plausible, even valid, in service of their relationship.

Bullsh*t can be thought of along any number of dimensions: insincere to sincere, nonsensical to serious, innocuous to harmful, tactical to strategic, tension reducing to tension raising—each serving any number of purposes. For instance, bullsh*t can be useful in communicating the strength of a feeling, as when exaggerated promises and threats are made without serious intent to actually carry out what's being spoken. People making such bullsh*t utterances aren't *really* about to love you in the morning, lend you money, or never speak to you again.

Bullsh*t can be nonsensical and obviously insincere. It can be a lighthearted way to signal the communicator's belief that someone's thinking is ridiculous or a deft means of avoiding an argument. It can be used for good-natured, playful, and irreverent bantering that encourages bonding. No one really expects to convince you to change your political party, swallow a live goldfish, or walk naked in a public place to win a bet. Bullsh*t utterances can raise tensions or reduce them. Tensions may be raised if you find someone disrespectfully beating around the bush on a matter you've asked about directly. Or tensions may be reduced, as when someone's obfuscation helps the two of you past an issue that can't be reconciled—perhaps one that could lead to the relationship rupturing if discussed seriously. One could go on and on describing the myriad forms and uses of such innocuous bullsh*t.

COVERT BULLSH*T

But when bullsh*t is covert it readily becomes insidious. *Covert bullsh*t* is my label for words spoken and actions taken that have no obvious relevance or apparent connection to the topic at hand. These words are spoken and actions taken to advance a hidden agenda on a topic that's not under discussion, a topic that may never be explicitly raised. Covert bullsh*t also covers instances when words essential to the communicator's agenda are *not* spoken or actions implied by that agenda, even agreed on by the parties, are not taken.[2] I use the descriptor *insidious* because of the anger that usually follows when a recipient later realizes a self-interested agenda was worked on them without their realizing it at the time. People don't like being fooled and they resent being manipulated by hidden persuaders.[3]

Like all bullsh*t, the *covert* form is not guided by what the communicator knows to be true. Unlike the overt form, the topic, agenda, and motivation of covert bullsh*t is kept under wraps and may appear irrelevant to what's being discussed in the moment. Forms of covert bullsh*t include name-dropping, ingratiating behavior, what-you-can-do-for-me relationship building, credential flaunting, maintaining face, grandstanding—the list is endless.[4] Because these manipulative communications are indirect and camouflaged, the communicator can plausibly deny any intent to mislead or manipulate. This plausible deniability is a key characteristic of covert bullsh*t, and the reason it can be so dangerous.

Covert bullsh*t entails pretense, illusion, process, and subliminal communication. It is designed to serve the communicator's interests on matters often far more important to the communicator than the ostensible topic on the table. Most of the time the communicator's interest is to get the person addressed to support his or her agenda or at least to stop resisting it. Sometimes covert bullsh*t entails a "two-ball billiard shot" communication. Then the communication is based on the premise that what's said and done will be retold to a second person who is the actual target of the influence. It makes little difference whether the bullsh*t is expressed as a serious, casual, or throwaway comment—in every instance the defining characteristic of covert bullsh*t is its one-sided, self-interested, camouflaged intent to advance the communicator's agenda.

Covert bullsh*t contrasts with overt bullsh*t much as *marketing* contrasts with *sales*. *Sales* is focused on making a real-time, here-and-now appeal that leads to a cash-currency, signature-on-the-dotted-line exchange for a specific product or service. In contrast, marketing is aimed at promoting the mind-set that the product, service, or brand is meritorious, valuable, and even life-enhancing. Similar to marketing, covert bullsh*t tries to induce recipients to orient in ways that may or not benefit them but always benefits the communicator.

Like marketing, covert bullsh*t comes in many varieties and is often attractively wrapped. However stylish the presentation, covert bullsh*t often backfires by leaving the recipient with the unpleasant feeling of having been taken in and manipulated. That recognition may not come quickly, however. (People often buy from a favorite product line without realizing why they chose it.) The recipient's eventual displeasure or disappointment depends on how long it takes to discover the manipulation and whether resultant harm can be undone.

As noted earlier, senders of covert bullsh*t readily hide behind a cloak of "plausible deniability." When exposed, they defend themselves against accusations of manipulation and selfishness on the grounds that it was never their intent to mislead, distort, miscommunicate, or self-promote. In the face of such denials, self-serving intent is almost impossible to prove. Accusers sense what took place, but having only circumstantial evidence of it, they are quickly stymied. Their accusations may be met with statements like "Oh, that's not at all what I meant to say," "I never thought you'd think that," "How can you possibly believe I would intentionally . . . ?" At the end of the day there may be increased surveillance or skepticism of the bullsh*t sender but this will diminish with time. Why shouldn't it? There's no proven violation. All that transpired was business as usual.

In both overt and covert bullsh*t, the driving force is the communicator's desire to persuade. When bullsh*t is covert, the communicator tries to get the recipient's support with little or no real interest in whether the agenda benefits them. Such communications are often spontaneous, with no thoughtful vetting for truthfulness on the communicator's part. The appeal is composed and orchestrated mainly to establish the context and mind-set that will entice the recipient to go along and even to play an active role in supporting the communicator's agenda.

Whether bullsh*t is overt or covert, you'll find it often plays a constructive role in daily organizational life, a role that most people fail to value at the time. Very importantly, it serves to support otherwise

Without bullsh*t, the workplace would be about as serene as the lawless Wild West.

meaningless protocol and pretense and to keep the corporate peace. Without bullsh*t, the workplace would be about as serene as the lawless Wild West. That's what the next chapter will explain.

3 BULLSH*T

It's Essential to Corporate Harmony

The head oncology researcher at a major university teaching and research hospital called for sounding-board advice. He was wondering how he might persuasively frame his pitch to be included on the Medical Review Oversight Team. He thought the committee should be expanded to include an oncology specialist, reasoning that cancer patients have unique needs requiring extraordinary considerations. Of course, he personally wanted the assignment and had a convincing argument for why he would be an outstanding selection. Besides, inclusion would give him visibility for administrative promotions and an enhancement in pay. But he feared contacting the director of research directly would sound self-serving, causing even his argument for the team's expansion to lack credibility.

I responded, "Easy. Just get a highly credible person from outside of oncology to pitch the concept and name you the logical candidate. That person might even say it was a conversation with you that spurred them to think an oncology expert would be an essential addition."

EVERYONE works with a "dirty little secret" that they know never to explicitly acknowledge to anyone but their closest friends. What's the secret? That self-interest, not organizational contribution, is the primary driving force behind every action taken at work. In other words, the world of work is a self-interested world in which individual motives and self-serving biases are embedded in an individual's every action and perception. However, owning up to these everyday manifestations of human nature can become an insurmountable personal liability. Associates will allege your advocacies are tainted even though they operate in much the same way themselves.

Acknowledging that self-interests drive your actions can destroy your ability to accomplish what's most important in the moment and even harm the credibility you need to reach future goals.[1] Exposed, self-interests provide others with a justification for discrediting your agenda on the grounds that what you are advocating as good for the organization is really primarily good for you. Of course, someone's desire to expose another's self-interested bias will be based, in large part, on their own self-serving agendas—not what is best for the company.

Once you understand this principle of human nature, you can utilize a little bullsh*t to make it work for you. That's what the oncology researcher at the beginning of this chapter did. He took my advice and found a third-party advocate who praised him into a spot on the oversight team. By the time the oncologist was on board, the director believed the decision was his idea, so successful was the oblique and mutually beneficial manipulation.

Despite its bad reputation, bullsh*t is the mechanism that the human race finds indispensable for obscuring the fact that self-interests, not organization interests, are the primary drivers. Bullsh*t enables you to portray self-interested pursuits as objectively mandated by the situation and serving the collective good. It allows you to create and maintain the façade that organizational priorities drive your actions. Bullsh*t is essential for communicating that the personal twists you impose on work agendas are necessary; that methods that "coincidentally" play to your strong suits are required; and

> Bullsh*t is the mechanism that the human race finds indispensable for obscuring the fact that self-interests, not organization interests, are the primary drivers.

that facts you cite to justify what you are doing and how you are doing it, are determined primarily and even exclusively, by a desire to propel company interests ahead. Of course, advancing company's interests is satisfying in and of itself—that is, if you get credit for doing so.

Bullsh*t maintains pretense. It allows you to pretend your analysis was rational, not emotional; your thinking was objective; and your actions were performed without bias or personal loyalties that might compromise what's best for the company. It is also the "schmooze" that allows you to politely tell another that you can't go along with their proposal, instead of insultingly blurt out that you find their proposal ineffective, poorly timed, ill conceived, or just plain self-indulgent.

In order to make your "objective," good-for-the-company portrayals sound convincing, you've first got to bullsh*t yourself. Only after you've made yourself a firm believer, can you, without deceit, deception, manipulation, or lying that's apparent, convince others of your dedication to the organization's cause. In other words, if you couldn't convince yourself that your self-interests and the organization's are one, you couldn't convincingly sell your agenda to others.

Thus, the world of work presents us with a bizarre situation: the need to package idiosyncratic self-interested pursuits as organizationally essential actions. And for this, bullsh*t is perfectly designed to be the communication etiquette of choice. Lying wouldn't work. The threat of discovery would evoke too much anxiety, and lies uncovered could lead to instant, even irrevocable, discrediting. Talking straight is risky because it can lead to revelations of self-interested motives, rendering the communicator vulnerable to accusations of selfishness and misappropriation of power. Someone with a competing agenda could call "foul," citing the compelling evidence you provided them.

Without bullsh*t to ease the frictions, organizational life would be unhealthily moralistic and excessively politically correct. Extreme oversight would be the norm. People would be constantly accused of commandeering organizational resources for self-serving gain, and the accusers countercharged as the accused self-defend. Without bullsh*t, every action would be scrutinized for self-advancing agendas, favoritism, self-indulgence, and inflation of personal contribution. Critical operations would come to a halt. Of course, given a self-interested world, such scrutiny takes place all the time. But thanks to bullsh*t, different views about what's the best organizational approach *are* argued purely on grounds of what's rational, objective, and organizationally effective as if the desire to succeed and other personal interests don't affect every word spoken and action taken. Such pretense represents institutionalized, mainstream-culture bullsh*t.

It's commonplace for people to express frustration when an issue that should take three minutes to decide sparks an arduous four-hour meeting, often without resolution.[2] What the frustrated fail to recognize is that the apparent inefficiency results from participants not being able to directly discuss their personal stakes in the matter that's on the table. One person's "objective" portrayal of organizational need clashes with someone else's slightly different "objective" portrayal. The debate escalates into infighting and deadlocks. Meanwhile, the personal issues underlying different proposals are never engaged directly.

Listening to words alone you'd never figure out how to resolve the matter. Usually the answer is an exchange of bullsh*t that lasts long enough for participants to hit on a commonly acceptable plan of what needs to be done. This consensus plan evolves as each person repackages their self-interested proposal into a compromise agreement ostensibly about what the organization "actually requires." Occasionally impasses are broken as a result of subliminal communication promising an offsetting benefit to be redeemed by a conceding party at a future date. Occasionally the conflict escalates to the point where avoidance of retribution and punishment is seen as a gain by parties who then concede.

There's a saying that never in the history of "mankind" did anyone ever wash a rental car. Likewise, never in the history of "personkind" did anyone ever propose an organizational move that they, at the time, failed to think was self-beneficial. This is the essence of bullsh*t. If someone proposes "a good" for the organization, you can rest assured that that "good" has at least passed the "good for me" test. Yet to be determined is the extent to which the organization's interests are being addressed and whether the proposed good includes positives for the others who will be affected. (Shortly I'll explain how such a determination can best be made in a straight-talk relationship.)

By now the cat should be out of the bag. There's far more diversity in the directions people take in the name of doing what's "objectively" required than the prevailing work culture has the capacity to recognize. The diversity results from nuanced differences in self-interested pursuits. Inevitably these differences emerge and clash as people only dimly aware of their self-interested motives elicit teamwork and cooperation from others, equally blind to the fact that they

> There's far more diversity in the directions people take in the name of doing what's "objectively" required than the prevailing work culture has the capacity to recognize.

are biased contributors. People adept at spotting other people's bullsh*t often don't recognize it in themselves.

We must not leave the topic of "Why the need for bullsh*t" without mentioning the bullsh*t required to impress evaluators who use metrics at odds with how you act and think. Too often they use standards that don't relate to the unique skill set you use to perform effectively, and they are inclined to frame your limitations as core deficiencies. I'm talking about the bullsh*t it takes to satisfy a boss who thinks you shouldn't be wasting your time performing tasks you find essential or the bullsh*t required to get an associate to change methods and priorities to better match what you think you need to do your job effectively. I'm talking about the daily bullsh*t required to make what you do for subjective reasons appear objective and necessary; to impress people on criteria you find unimportant; to demonstrate loyalty to someone who hasn't been loyal to you; to indicate that your area of expertise is essential; to document that you're promotion worthy; to demonstrate you are in the political fold when you are not. I'm even referring to the bullsh*t you use in convincing yourself that you don't fit a bum rap stereotype laid on you years ago by someone no longer in your life—as when you try to prove to a long dead parent that you are not the selfish child he or she thought you were.

I'm talking about the constant flow of bullsh*t required to deal with people who get to evaluate you without your being able to comment directly on the inappropriateness of the criteria they use in passing judgment. This is a situation that I've researched thoroughly and refer to as one-sided accountability and hierarchical pretense. As far as I'm concerned it's a culturally imposed curse that, until you find the means to counter it, will constantly impede your functioning. This was the prime topic of my last book, *Don't Kill the Bosses!* I address this culturally imposed myopia next, in Chapter 4. And I take it up a final time in Chapter 8 by showing how standard evaluation processes, rife with bullsh*t, impede straight-talk and teamwork between bosses and their direct reports.

4

BULLSH*T

Corporate Pretense Cancels Human Nature

The director of technical support (TS) gave his "enhancements-underway" report at the annual managerial retreat and had moved on to Q&A. Not seeing the raised hand of Jack, a service manager who often complains about the inability of TS functionaries to provide the support he's looking for, the COO tapped him on the shoulder and whispered, "Don't you chicken out." This prompted Jack to ask a "When are we going to have the ability to . . ." question, referring to a simple refinement that would produce significant bottom-line savings. The answer was a noncommittal, "That's also on our list," with no date of completion or priority in the queue provided.

Later on, at a stand-up reception, the COO overheard Jack bragging, "I sure let them have it and, as usual, they gave us a bullsh*t response." The COO reacted with astonishment. In measured tones he said, "That may be, but apparently that's your game too. I don't think TS knows you let them have anything. Once again, I think you chickened out." Then the COO asked, "Do you think you'd get the same answer if you provided even ballpark numbers documenting in dollars what you are *alleging their unresponsiveness is costing the company?" Jack looked for a table to crawl under but couldn't find one. That was the moment he discovered the COO had long been onto him without his being onto himself.*

I'VE DEFINED BULLSH*T as words spoken or actions taken with the goal of getting people to go along with an agenda without the communicator giving serious consideration to the veracity of the communication. I'd now like to add another element to that definition. Bullsh*t is usually dispensed without serious consideration for its impact on the agendas of the targeted recipients. Usually there's no malice of forethought and no intent to deceive. The communicator is merely following standard corporate practices. Nevertheless, recipients commonly end up feeling deceived.

That was the case with both Jack and the director of technical support in the story that opened this chapter. Although Jack didn't realize it, his interaction with technical support was as much a "bullsh*t" response as what he accused TS of. He never considered their need for more information to answer his questions meaningfully. By calling Jack on his bullsh*t, the COO paved the way for more meaningful interdepartmental communication in the future.

If you probe people using bullsh*t, you'll find most were unaware of what they were doing and even unaware that their messages were being read as bullsh*t. Absorbed in persuading and soliciting support, few people take time to realize what they overlooked in the moment. In fact, just recently a high-level manager assured me "I no longer resort to bullsh*t." He said, "I now take pains to begin each meeting by telling the group precisely what I want." I thought, "Does he really think what he wants is, by definition, valid for everyone in the room? Does he really think lower-level people trust him enough to speak up and set him straight about their different points of view?"

In action, few people see themselves as less than up front. Few realize they occasionally tell more than a benign white lie. Few see themselves omitting essential facts, exaggerating the truth for impact, overzealously trying to convince, being self-conveniently vague, out to create false impressions, breaking commitments, or attributing their own motives to others. But it's common for people to replay their actions, especially after others complain they were misled. It is only then that they realize what more they might have done to rigorously communicate the facts and truths they knew at the time.

But subsequent reflection on bullsh*t dispensed rarely results in the communicators backtracking to recast their self-serving agendas more candidly and accurately. Even when they see their flaws, most people self-exonerate or laugh. Sometimes they admit "I guess I got a little carried away." Sometimes they self-justify, rationalizing "We were in a jam, quick action was needed, and, out of necessity, there was no other course I could take." They rarely feel the kind of angst that leads to setting-the-record-straight amends.

Because overt bullsh*t is so common in the workplace, people are inured to it. They don't vigorously object, most of the time, to being on the receiving end as long as the communicator's agenda is presented in a discussable format. There's little need to object when you know the topic, can follow the appeals, and see yourself as having a measure of control. You can agree when it's in your interest, disagree when it's not, and negotiate for alternatives that best serve you. Of course, all your comments will reflect the ostensible goal of doing what's best for "organizational effectiveness." That's how the system works.

On the other hand, one seldom encounters recipients of covert bullsh*t who aren't distressed when they discover they have been subliminally persuaded to support an agenda that worked against their self-interests. Even people whose self-interested goals are served by the communicator's covert agenda get upset when they realize a persuasive message was sent clandestinely. Their distress goes beyond feeling that somebody put one over on them. It's also about being denied the opportunity to listen with a "buyer-beware" mentality. In a self-interested world where self-interests can't be explicitly discussed, each person feels obliged to patrol for opportunities gained and lost, tracking events from the point of view of "what does this do for me?" People respond negatively to stealth influences, once they are exposed, as they wonder what else has been or will be slipped by them.

Examining communications to sort the bullsh*t from the chafe (sic) is more readily accomplished when you accept the fact that the world of work is a self-interested world. If you forget that, it's easy to miss self-interested bullsh*t, especially when it comes from someone you have yet to categorize as "always talking bullsh*t." Many of us can recount times we got taken in by an initiative that was illogical from the beginning. We've gone along with evaluation systems, like 360-degree feedback, that in context made little sense. We've hired people we knew wouldn't work out. We've accepted organizational practices that made getting results more difficult. We've attended meetings we knew could only waste our time. Alternatively, we occasionally have caught someone red-handed, using rhetoric clearly intended to put one over on us. Confronting that person with "smoking gun" evidence only caused them to be more artful in communicating bullsh*t, casting their offensive action as serving the corporate good.

A "positivistic" work culture makes it more difficult to keep track of bullsh*t directed your way. Ours is a culture that emphasizes progress in the face of all obstacles and disdains inaction. Such a culture produces the inclination to excuse and ignore interpersonal moments we don't understand. It's a culture that readily puts people down for being too analytical, too emotional, too psychologically focused, or too caught up with political issues that can't be dealt with expeditiously. We try to avoid puzzling about a proposal that doesn't seem quite right or talking about what's bothersome without being able to point to something tangible. In our culture it's a plus to project a self-confident "can-do" image. It's a negative to be seen mulling over vague misgivings lest others conclude "weakness," "indecisiveness," "negativity," "suspiciousness," or "distraction."

The need to demystify communications becomes especially strong when you sense that the topic on the table is not the actual issue being transacted—when you feel, in other words, you are the target of covert bullsh*t. At such moments your instincts and intuition send messages that, lacking a plausible interpretation, your intellect wants to dismiss. You know something is off. But you are intimidated, afraid what's off might be you. You begin to question whether you're forgetting something you've already been told. You suspect you need better surveillance skills.

Almost anything can sound your alarm, causing you to probe for subliminal influences. You may hear emotion you find unwarranted, can't place, or believe to be overblown. You may hear words that don't quite pertain to the topic you're discussing; you may view atypical behavior in another. Or perhaps you're asked to a meeting at times or places that seem odd; you get calls from people you don't expect to hear from; you receive compliments you find excessive; someone intimate turns aloof; someone distant appears chummy; people assume things about you that you find surprising; criteria for results don't align with actions taken. In short, something about the content, relationship, emotions, context, or physical event fails to square with precedent or your expectations. You feel something is off, even if you can't quite specify what it is. But, short of total skepticism and abject paranoia, how do you develop the internal radar to detect the disguised self-serving agendas of other people?

When scanning for covert agendas most people take an intuitive approach. They rely on gut instinct and other feelings to tell them whether more is taking place than meets their eyes. Sometimes people augment their intuition with open-ended questions like, "What am I missing here?" They ask associates who might know more, "Why do you suppose succession planning was mentioned in this morning's meeting?" They send out trial balloons like, "That came from out of the blue for me. How did you understand what happened?" Then, they carefully listen to the other person's response. Unfortunately proceeding this way involves depending entirely on others. You're stuck relying on third parties and possible perpetrators of bullsh*t to reveal what they may not want you, or even themselves, to know.

Many people don't realize that they can enhance their ability to uncover what's not immediately apparent. Sometimes they quickly sense what someone is up to covertly but lack the confidence to act. Hesitation is understandable. After all, behavior doesn't speak for itself. Understanding what's covert first requires figuring out the intent behind the behavior. Without knowing what a person is trying to accomplish, it's difficult to respond appropriately.

You'll find your ability to discern intent increased considerably if you keep the basics of human nature in focus. First, as I've already emphasized, the world of work is a self-interested world. But it's also a world where people justify whatever they want to do on grounds that it's organizationally essential.

Second, everything a person says or does stems from a desire to live a personally meaningful life and succeed on personally relevant criteria. While work is a very important aspect of life, it's not the only one. Most of the time, despite what people say, what they do at work is dictated by other, more important life pursuits, personal history, and home-situation dilemmas.

Third, what's personally meaningful and what constitutes "success" are determined by intrinsic factors, distinctive as an individual's thumbprint. Indeed, for the individual, nothing taking place at work has much meaning outside of what he or she ascribes to it.

Fourth, to be human is to be imperfect. No one comes equipped with every competency and at no point are all basic lessons learned. Personal effectiveness requires drawing from an uneven repertoire of imperfect skills and making successful applications. A person's effectiveness depends on reinterpreting assignments to better fit their competencies, interests, and personal definitions of meaning and accomplishment. Because no action speaks for itself and each person largely creates their own reality, you don't know the meaning of anything a person says or does until you know their intent.

Most people are vaguely aware of all of this and have everyday experiences that verify it. But few people get all the insight they should from knowing these basics. At critical moments they disconnect from what they know about human nature. That wouldn't happen if these principles of human behavior were hardwired in their minds the way the rules of mathematics are. If someone says $2 + 2 = 5$, people instantly know that's not correct. This is how it should be with such human verities as the inevitability of self-interest, personal quests for meaning, diversity in personal agendas, and individual modes of operating based on individual competencies. But the collective pretenses that organizations maintain, notably the fiction that everything is done to serve the company and that corporate assumptions and practices are rational and objective cause people to disconnect from the basic things they know about human nature.

The difficulty people have in using what they know comes from getting caught up in these collective pretenses. It's one thing for people to choose to "go along to get along" in some situations. It's another to lose track of human nature when going along. That's the equivalent of forgetting that 2 + 2 = 4 when others insist 5 is the right answer. The conundrum is: How to talk straight to people who aren't thinking straight about themselves?

TECHNIQUE: SELF-CONFRONTATION

I've put a great deal of effort into developing methods that help MBA students overcome their tendency to disconnect from what they know about human nature. Minimally, I try to help them see how easily they lose their bearings when caught up in the shared illusions and collective pretenses of most organizations. For example, look at how often people measure their contribution to an organization on an externally imposed metric that is irrelevant to the situation being faced or the unique way that individual works most effectively. For example, look at how readily people who earned A's in "business ethics" were able to rationalize the blatantly unethical actions they took part in when working at Enron and Arthur Andersen.

For example, consider how readily bosses blame performance problems on subordinates doing things they would never do except to please those bosses.

I'm constantly on the lookout for set-breakers. Finding them is core to my work. I wonder what experience, what recalibration of thinking, might equip people to resist disconnecting from what they most basically know when they feel compelled to go along with corporate

> I wonder what experience, what recalibration of thinking, might equip people to resist disconnecting from what they most basically know when they feel compelled to go along with corporate protocol that has them speaking bullsh*t?

protocol that has them speaking bullsh*t? How can they keep their knowledge of human nature in focus while maintaining a pretense of objectivism and rationality? Knowledge of human nature tells us that there are no "one-size-fits-all" answers. Overcoming the tendency to disconnect is something each person has to master in a unique way.

I have developed a method that I currently use in getting students to internalize this critical lesson. That method entails a term-long "setup" culminating in self-confrontation. I do my best to get students to relate emotionally to this lesson in order to ensure its impact. The setup entails premeditated deception that could mistakenly be seen as "covert bullsh*t." That's because my goal is persuasion, and I'm not immediately up front either in presenting my agenda or acknowledging my methodology. But I don't think of it as covert bullsh*t, I think of it as "tough love" teaching.

The venue is a leadership course that emphasizes the value of paying attention to established principles of human nature. Students are expected to take stock of their leadership strengths and weaknesses and to acquire skills for effectively engaging people who operate differently. The set-breaking moment takes place in a concluding session that comes immediately after the final exam. It's a wrap-up session during which I tell students the answers I'm inclined to grade as "correct" and give them the opportunity to argue the validity of what they put down on the test. The discussion I'm counting on to provoke self-confrontation takes place at the very end. It involves an innocuous-appearing short question that I've spent the term setting up for dramatic impact.

In my experience, over 90 percent of the students will not give the "correct" answer, although, given the orientation of the course, everyone should have gotten it right. The question vividly underscores how easily students can disconnect from what they know about human nature when in an everyday situation steeped in corporate protocol and pretense. I want students to think about the real-world consequences of any disconnect, and I want the lesson to become etched indelibly in their minds. To that end, I tell them that those who answer this question correctly will automatically receive an "A" grade for the entire exam. Here's the question I pose:

You miss a scheduled meeting with a woman with whom you regularly conduct business. In response she leaves an extremely angry voice-mail threatening to end her dealings with you. Use your knowledge of human nature to analyze her behavior in understanding why and how her actions arose. Then tell what you are going to say when the two of you eventually talk.

I use the 15-minute break between the exam and the wrap-up to compile a sample of incorrect test answers to read out loud to the class. After reading an answer, I invite the author to explain the reasoning behind it. I then ask, "Did anyone get to the same place following a different line of reasoning?" After a number of students have explained their answers, I suddenly switch roles. Exit "understanding professor." Enter "Sultan of Wac-A-Mole." In contrast to the tone of the rest of the session, I engage in exaggerated tongue-in-cheek chiding, mocking the disconnected reasoning in the answers I have just read. Feigning seriousness, I say, "There'll be no stay of execution for people who committed this capital crime."

I tell students, "There's only one answer I'm prepared to grade correct. It's your variation on a theme that can be expressed in three short words: 'You don't know.' It's what we've been talking about all quarter. You know almost nothing about this person so you don't know what caused her anger. It may not even relate to what you did. Even if her words were prompted by your mistake, you still don't know what life history and personal traits connect her 'extreme' reaction to your 'modest' slip up. It could be unresolved frustration with an older sister who never gave her the time of day; maybe she spilled coffee on her laptop while she was calling you. It could be just about anything. You don't now know enough to speculate. In order to find out, you'll have to ask her."

At this point I'm expecting stunned silence, since the lesson inevitably evokes strong emotions, but I can never predict how the students will respond. I also know that a strong emotional response is only the beginning point for self-confrontation. Intellect needs to follow. If the students respond with silence, I let the silence run its course. If their response is boisterous, I let them "boister" about. Then I describe how I set up the situation and why this lesson is so important. I share my rationale for the grading procedure. I ask the students: "What's the value of getting an A on book knowledge you don't apply?" I go on, "When it comes to relating to human nature, you owe yourself an A on the practicum." I urge students to be self-confronting each time they catch themselves disconnected from what they know about human nature. I have no way of determining how many people immediately internalize the lesson or how many eventually will. But it's very gratifying to receive e-mails from former students describing how important the class was to them and, in particular, the value of this term-ending "tough-love" lesson.

Going along with accepted protocol typically requires speaking rationalistic bullsh*t. People say what they need to say to get support for their agendas and to avoid other people's resistance. But it's one thing to follow the prescribed format. It is something else entirely to get so involved in a format that you disconnect from the fundamental truths you know about yourself and others. Disconnecting means telling covert bullsh*t to the one individual you never want to deceive: yourself. Maintaining your bearings and staying lucid in the face of bullsh*t requires you to engage in a process I call truth-finding.

Truth-finding contrasts sharply with what gets accomplished with bullsh*t. Bullsh*t mystifies. It disconnects behavior from intent; it omits critical facts and fails to consider other people and their self-interested agendas in pursuit of one's own. In contrast, truth-finding demystifies. It utilizes knowledge of human nature, both universal and facts specific to the other person, to discover their intent and reveal the underlying meaning of their communications. The very good news here is that there are many constructive techniques you can take to demystify situations you find puzzling. Two truth-finding approaches are described in Chapter 11. The next chapter, Chapter 5, describes what's required for straight-talk. The chapter will help you maintain your bearings in the midst of the bullsh*t typical of every organization. And it will show you how straight-talk can be your anchor.

THEORY SECTION — STRAIGHT-TALK

5

STRAIGHT-TALK
I-Speak Required

In a discussion with his management consultant, Stan (the CEO) said, "My mind is made up. I'm going to fire Peter (the COO) and I don't want you telling him." Asked why, Stan responded, "Because from the beginning I've been on his case to bring in strong people. It's reached the point where Peter alone is driving all significant activities. All operating success, and grant you it's been substantial, is directly due to Peter. But his mode of operating is killing our organization. We could be doing so much more if he had only brought in strong leaders."

Loyal to Peter, perhaps to a fault, the consultant said, "Give him a month. I'll help you get the message across and then, if he wants, I'll help Peter with the hiring." Reiterating that his mind was firmly made up, Stan conceded that he had no replacement identified so there still might be time. Stan also warned that only the consultant knew his thinking and that he alone would be held accountable for any confidentiality breach.

That night the consultant called Peter to report on "a conversation I had with Stan today." Conscious of the admonition not to break confidence, he said, "I'm so frustrated! I went in to tell Stan about all the good things you're accomplishing and he wouldn't listen to a thing I was saying. All he wanted to talk about were his frustrations that you haven't hired senior people. This time I think you've got to drop everything and give Stan what he wants. I don't think you've got a moment to spare."

IT'S TAKEN SEVERAL CHAPTERS to lay the foundation for presenting a definition of straight-talk that's precise enough for practical use. Of course, you'll have to think degrees of straight-talk since, in this, as in all matters of human discourse, there are no absolutes. In calibrating your straight-talk, you will want to consider cultural differences, comfort with intimacy, organizational context, preferences in communication style, and perhaps most important, the certainty that you and the people with whom you are talking straight will see each situation uniquely—through the prisms of your respective minds. Your decision on how straight you want to talk will be based on the answers to such questions as how much honesty, on what topics, with what implications for actions to be taken, as seen and judged by whom, and under what circumstances will the interaction take place.

Because Frankfurt's essay *On Bullshit* doesn't touch on straight-talk, it doesn't distinguish straight-talk from *lying* and *bullsh*t*. However, making these distinctions helped clarify the subject for me, and I want to share that analysis with you now. Contemplating the distinctions allowed me to identify two of the three defining features of straight-talk.

Most people consider straight-talk to be the opposite of *lying*, and this is a primary defining feature. As with lying, straight-talk requires serious consideration of the truth the communicator knows. But in lying, focusing on the truth-one-knows is a prelude to deception. In contrast, in straight-talk, the speaker focuses on the truth-one-knows in order to conduct self-interested pursuits with both inner and other-directed integrity.

Inner integrity is important to straight-talk. People need to scrutinize the basis of their beliefs. Those who haven't vetted the truth for their own consumption cannot tell high-quality truths to others. However, not all vetting of truth for self-consumption is the same. Sometimes it's casual reflection; sometimes it's brutally honest soul-searching. Many factors are involved: the individual's motivation, interest in the topic, the politics of the moment, personal capacity, and the like. Furthermore, no external communication is independent of how the communicator sizes up the recipient's interests, mentality, needs to know, and what's required in the way of the "Kentucky windage,"[1] that is adjustments to ensure message-received accuracy and the impact that's desired.

> Those who haven't vetted the truth for their own consumption cannot tell high-quality truths to others.

One recognizes the second defining feature of straight-talk in distinguishing it from bullsh*t. Like bullsh*t, straight-talk is directed at eliciting support for self-interested agendas. But, unlike those who bullsh*t, people in a straight-talk relationship are also concerned with the self-interested pursuits and well-being of the people they want to persuade.

That is not to say that straight-talk entails putting other people's interests ahead of one's own. It merely means that straight-talk includes the boilerplate agreement that underlies all collaborative relationships: concern for the operational effectiveness and personal well-being of others on your team. This requires giving open-minded consideration to how the agendas being pursued affect the self-interests of the people whose support is being solicited, with energy spent on finding out what those interests are.

Whereas bullsh*t entails one-sided, buyer-beware advocacy, straight-talk entails two-sided, reciprocally accountable partnering. Cohorts recognize that what their partner has concluded to be true results from experiences they know little about. They expend energy inquiring about the goals and agendas of the other person and the powerful life experiences that account for them. If money and status is the other person's goal, the straight-talker might inquire into what life events make these rewards so important to the other person. In straight-talk, an attempt is made to synergize personal agendas in an effort to help each participant succeed. The parties consider the others' personal well-being and goals that don't directly benefit themselves. In short, unlike bullsh*t, straight-talk entails learning what others are up to and helping them realize their agendas whenever possible.

The third defining feature of straight-talk is its moral/ethical, non-conspiratorial nature. Whatever fantasies and irreverent ideas are exchanged by sharers of straight-talk, its ultimate outcome should be ethically and morally valid for the organization as a whole, and advance legitimate institutional goals. The outcomes should do no harm to others on the team who will be affected but are not in the room to advocate for themselves. Straight-talk includes recognizing the interests of the work entity as a community of interests. It's not straight-talk when the end result of two people talking candidly is the domination of others on the team, personal gain at their expense, ethnocentric advantage, or marketplace dishonesty. That type of behavior constitutes *collusion* or even *conspiracy*.

Some people confuse straight-talk with a one-sided, core-dump opportunity to vent frustrations. They self-indulgently blurt out truths-they-know as if there were no other valid way to describe reality. In this regard I'm reminded of the often-cited scripture: "The truth will set you free." Maybe truth handed down by God and verified by science will set us free. But in daily affairs we're not talking about any absolute "truth" of that sort. Instead we are talking about an idiosyncratic "truth-as-I-understand-it-and-think-it-to-be," often made even more idiosyncratic by the particular circumstances in which the alleged truth-telling occurs. In such cases, what the speaker describes as truth may really be a means of steamrolling over perceived obstacles. Truths told for such purposes, without concern and consideration for the recipient's agenda and well-being, do not qualify as straight-talk.

Straight-talk is more rigorous than truth-telling. While there are many reasons to tell the truth, there's only one underlying reason for straight-talk: self- and other-integrity. Truth-telling entails *power-taking*—you state reality as you see it and implicitly challenge the other person either to join with you or prove you wrong. In contrast, straight-talk entails *power-sharing*—you state your reality while recognizing that the other person probably sees things differently. Implied is an invitation for the others to also put their views and interests on the table in order to identify differences and discover what modifications in each agenda might harmonize the self-interests involved.

Truth-telling involves one-sided accountability—you share your truth expecting the other person to back the conclusions, agenda, and goals implied. Straight-talk entails two-sided accountability—you extend support for the other person's agenda, provide guidance on how he or she might be more effective, are concerned for their general well-being, and expect comparable consideration in return. When your positions conflict, you are mutually responsible for finding a realignment that addresses one another's needs. When one person in a straight-talk relationship doesn't know how to back the other's agenda, without abandoning an important self-interest, that person is expected to say so up front. That can be accomplished with a simple statement such as, "I don't know how to incorporate your interests in what I'm proposing. If you see a way to do so, I'd like to hear about it."

Straight-talk is different from *lying*, an action taken to advance oneself, which may or may not directly benefit anyone else: a *win* for self. It is different from *bullsh*t*, an action taken to produce a win for self, justified on the grounds that it produces a win for the corporation: a *win-win*. Straight-talk has the potential to make everyone a winner. Straight-talk advances, or at least does not obstruct, the interests of other stakeholders by respecting the moral/ethical contract that characterizes progressive societies. As such, straight-talk has the potential to produce a win for self, a win for the cohorts, and a win for the organization and its stakeholders: a *win-win-win*.

Unlike straight-talk, truth-telling can help the organization or be a weapon that harms. As writer and women's rights advocate Gloria Steinem observed, paraphrasing the previously cited scripture: "The truth may set you free. But first it will *piss* you off." With that in mind, I'm limiting the term straight-talk to situations in which both the communicator and recipient recognize the fact that the truth-they-know is a self-biased representation. This means respecting that others—with unique life experiences, knowledge, sensitivities, and personal goals—have legitimate reasons for seeing and interpreting each event differently than you interpret it. Straight-talkers communicate this recognition by presenting their "truths" using *I-speak*—an acknowledgment that "this is the truth *I* distinctively know."

TECHNIQUE: I-SPEAK

"I-speak" is remarkable in its ability to let others know that what you are saying reflects what you, idiosyncratically, think. At the same time, it clearly implies that they may think something quite different—and have every right to do so. Even when you use the tonality of an oracle or an expert, I-speak implies that your thoughts are the product of personal experiences, life lessons learned, and acquired wisdom. In other words, it implies that yours is a self-created, even biased reality.

I-speak adds an "I think," "I see," "I believe," "I feel," "given my needs," "based on what I know," "in my judgment," "the way I view it," or "in my experience" to all recitations of fact and belief. Speaking this way leaves others room to express their different views. It avoids win-lose, right-wrong, who-is-objectively-correct arguments when people pursuing different self-interests clash. It implies a relationship of equality and a commitment to fair play.

The opening story illustrates how effective and subtle an instrument I-speak can be. By referring to his own frustration, the management consultant was able to warn Peter that his job was in danger. Ideal for sensitive conversations, I-speak allowed the consultant to do so without violating his promise to the CEO not to tell Peter he was about to be fired.

Used thoughtfully, I-speak contains one and one-half of the three defining features of straight-talk. It has the self-honesty component and recognition that the person addressed has a different set of interests and agendas and thus may see events differently than you see them. It leaves space for other people to state their views. I-speak does not necessarily imply that you have knowledge of the other person's interests or how that individual sees and interprets events. Nor does it necessarily acknowledge the ethical/moral needs of a greater community or system. At the same time, it doesn't preclude any of these requisites for straight-talk.

The use of I-speak acknowledges that every human being is different and, thus, each sees and interprets the world differently. I-speak communicates respect for that fact of human nature, and, in most instances, communicates an interest in hearing the views of others. Talking straight requires give-and-take communication and recognizes the fact that each person's views may remain different, no matter how hard they try to reconcile them.

As a practical matter, I-speak brings civility to touchy conversations, especially those bearing on subordinate performance and work results. For example, it is an invaluable tool during high-stress workplace events such as firings. Using I-speak you simply announce that you're exercising your prerogative to have the workplace equivalent of a no-fault divorce. Your words might parallel those of someone unilaterally deciding to quit for a better job. What's required is a statement such as, "I haven't been able to figure out how to get the results I want working with you. I want to see if I can achieve better chemistry working with someone else." This may feel overly euphemistic, but, in fact, may be an accurate statement. Think about it. Someone else in your position, perhaps your subordinate's last boss, would have worked differently with him or her. What's more, no useful purpose is served by handing the departing employee a list of insufficiencies at the very moment that the person most needs to feel worthwhile. How the individual could have done the job better is a conversation that should have been held earlier, when you and the company could have enjoyed the benefits of any improvement made.

Conversely, straight-talk is negated when a nonspecific, corporate "we" is used. Use of "we" implies that all the "right" people see it the way I see it, thereby inflating the status of "truth-as-*I*-see-it" to "truth-as-it-*objectively* exists." Even saying something as innocuous as "You just don't understand . . . " is far different than saying, "Your understanding of this situation and what should be done is quite different from mine." The former implies there's something deficient in the other person and their view, as if all the informed, rational, objective, cool people (you included) see it this way.

People pursuing work agendas with bullsh*t love the corporate "*we*." They use it to deftly undermine alternative viewpoints and perspectives by branding them inferior. "We" intimidates by implying that anyone thinking differently is "an outlier," stubbornly resisting the superior wisdom of the organization. The corporate "we" papers over the fact that your view is yours, not necessarily that of others in the company who may not have held a single conversation on the matter at hand. In such instances, the corporate "we" is a blunt instrument for overpowering other people.

To summarize, I define straight-talk as communication, in word and action, on a variety of agendas, in which self-interested parties seek to truthfully represent their views, with genuine concern for the agendas and well-being of others and collateral concern for the impact on the organization. Straight-talk includes willingness to consider modifications that would advance synergy and reciprocal success. It requires restraint in not proposing or taking actions that might harm team members not present, including individuals, organizational units, the organization as a whole, and even the larger community and society.

6 STRAIGHT-TALK
How Does It Differ from Truth-Telling and Candor?

Newly appointed Federal Reserve Chairman Ben Bernanke "acknowledged that he made a 'lapse in judgment' by discussing Federal Reserve policy with the CNBC television anchor—comments that subsequently drove the stock and bond prices lower." When asked about his comments during a session of the Senate Banking Committee, Bernanke candidly admitted his mistake, saying, "In the future, my communications with the public and with the markets will be entirely through regular and formal channels."[1] Apparently his straight to the point admission was sufficient to stem public outcry. To date, no heated criticism has appeared in the press nor have suits been filed by people claiming financial injury.

STRAIGHT-TALK is not a one-time conversation. It's not simply a candid spontaneous discussion. Rather it is a candid encounter in the context of a reciprocally supportive and caring relationship. Straight-talking cohorts give and expect reciprocal concern on almost any matter bearing on each other's work effectiveness and personal well-being. They expect honest "Here's-what-I-think-about-this" reactions on demand. Straight-talking cohorts are expected to initiate a discussion when they see a problem brewing for the other. Straight-talk differs from the other "honesty-sending" formats—truth-telling and candor.

I see three distinct types of "honesty" venues in the workplace. There are the truth-telling moment, the candid topical discussion, and the candor-on-demand straight-talk relationship. Each has its own characteristics. Truth-telling entails unilateral honesty and is specific to a moment; candor is marked by give-and-take honesty, is specific to a topic, and is usually episodic; and straight-talk is marked by bilateral honesty, is specific to a relationship, and is, for the most part, not exclusive to any one incident, episode, or topic. Some of the time truth-telling and candor spawn reciprocity that, over time, evolves into a straight-talk relationship with its bonds of trust, loyalty, confidentiality, and valuing the other that often leads to genuine friendship.

There's one other type of truth-telling, which could be labeled *circumstance-forced truth-telling*. This occurs when externals evoke an honesty that probably would not have been expressed if the speaker had more control over his or her emotions or the situation itself. This burst of honesty can be provoked by any number of external events, including testifying under oath, unbendable requirements of the job, personal revelations made to win someone's support, conversations while drinking, the breaking of barriers to candor such as the freedom to talk now that one has changed jobs, emotional release during traumatic events such as when one is fired, has a friend die, goes through a divorce, is caught in a suspicious seeming situation, loses "it" during a fit of anger, and the like. This type of truth-telling becomes bullsh*t when it results in the recipient erroneously concluding that a truth-on-demand relationship has been forged. While the possibility of an "all you have to do is ask and I'll tell you truthfully" relationship can never be discounted, one should not presume it exists simply because of another's apparent candor. Sometimes such honesty is simply the result of immediate circumstances.

Of the three bona fide honesty venues, truth-telling is most subject to an infusion of bullsh*t, and we've already covered some of what I think about this. Truth-telling is clearly a positive when you are raising important questions and the other person has an educated understanding of the agenda you're pursuing and the rationale for your questions. They are then positioned to craft a version of the truth-they-know that best conforms to your reasons for asking.

Of course, any version will have some spin. (Spin is a by-product of any speaker's self-interests.) A truth-telling communication can make the communicator or the recipient vulnerable. A message that makes the communicator vulnerable should be seen as a noble gesture, worthy of appreciation and respect. If the message only makes the recipient vulnerable, it is suspect at best and probably bullsh*t. Truth-telling becomes bullsh*t when the particular moment chosen for telling you something honestly is solely self-advantageous for the communicator, making you and your agenda, not them and their agenda, vulnerable.

> Truth-telling becomes bullsh*t when the particular moment chosen for telling you something honestly is solely self-advantageous for the communicator, making you and your agenda, not them and their agenda, vulnerable.

I view candor as an episodic, reciprocal, truth-as-one-knows-it, topical discussion and exchange. It usually occurs spontaneously as people with common interests feel an immediate need to get to the heart of some matter, perhaps out of desire to avoid an externally imposed penalty or due to pressure to achieve a deadline or goal. It's a cut-to-the-chase, let-the-chips-fall-where-they-may conversation in which participants deviate from their usual indirectness, pretense, and image management in order to openly and bluntly voice their views. There's a surface appearance of thoughtfulness and honesty and, indeed, that's often what's taking place. However, unless such conversations spring from a continuing personal relationship, you can't count on full-disclosure accountability on the part of the communicator. Candor leaves room for people to spin, misrepresent, and withhold facts and opinions that might undermine their ability to recruit support for positions they favor. Such "candor" constitutes bullsh*t or worse.

Candor is more extensive in scope than truth-telling. A candid conversation can entail an honest and spontaneous exchange of all relevant information and viewpoints, with minimal self-censoring for political correctness and intention, on a topic that each person deems sufficiently important at the time. In this sense, I don't believe you are truly having a candid discussion when you talk about the weather, a sporting event, or an individual irrelevant to your common interests (the last case being an example of what we usually term gossip). In other words, genuine candor doesn't occur unless self-interests, personal agendas, or interpersonal vulnerability is involved. I reserve the term *candor* for a conversation where two or more people communicate with an unusual amount of honesty, spontaneity, and clarity-seeking interest on a topic that's important to all of them.

Candid conversations are usually experienced as a welcome contrast to run-of-the-mill bullsh*t conversations. They can create good feelings and, irrespective of progress made, often lift people's spirits. Held on meaningful topics, they give participants the sense that they are building community with well-intentioned others who have information and viewpoints that will help them be more productive and benefit them in other ways. Candid interactions can be sources of believable information and knowledge exchange. They affirm people's hopes that efforts expended will reap results, thereby generating optimism. But as wonderful as candid conversations may feel, their long-term, team-building impact can be short-lived. Too often the only lasting result is single-topic *coalition building* that results from people divulging enough—where they are coming from, their desired ends, how they see events, conclusions they have reached—to align their individual positions on a single topic for mutual gain.

A candid conversation transcends bullsh*t only when "truths" germane to everyone in the group are included in the discussion. Such transcendence also depends on how the discussion is cast in each participant's mind once the conversation is over. When a discussion is perceived as having led to the acquiring of valuable information, reaching a goal or meeting a deadline, it rises to the level of candor, not bullsh*t. But candor that serves only fleeting convenience or is marked by substantive omission is really bullsh*t. Similarly, apparent candor that's represented as the product of a trusting, caring, and enduring friendship that doesn't yet exist is also bullsh*t. Politicians seem especially adept at purveying this variety: John McCain's 2004 public hugging and attempted kiss of George W. Bush, the same man whose dirty tricks scuttled McCain's bid for the Republican Party 2000 nomination immediately comes to mind. As noted previously, sometimes a candid discussion on a single topic eventually leads to a straight-talk relationship. But usually much more is required.

7

STRAIGHT-TALK
Relationship Is King

The unexamined life is not worth living.
—Socrates (Plato, *Apology* 38a)

Prior to adjournment I thanked Howard, the new board chairman, for the open-minded and fair way he ran the meeting. The next morning he surprised me with an e-mail stating, "I never feel comfortable with public compliments so I pushed yours away at the time. But it did register and I want you to know that I truly appreciated it. Particularly after all we've been through together. Thanks for noticing what I did." The note was posted at 12:30 A.M., which I read as evidence that my compliment had been important to him.

I forwarded the e-mail to Mel, the CEO, who had recruited me for the common shareholders' seat. Up until now neither of us had been impressed with Howard and had criticized him for divisive, polarizing politics, including an episode in which he unsuccessfully led a cabal to oust me. In response Mel phoned asking for clarification. "That was the only part of the meeting I didn't understand," Mel said. "Was your flattery sincere or was that all bullsh*t?"

Taking a moment, I reflected, "I was conscious of thinking it was, far and away, the best meeting we've had. I saw publicly complimenting Howard as an opportunity to do some relationship rebuilding. From his reaction I'd say it worked."

WHEN IT COMES TO STRAIGHT-TALK, relationship is king. We're talking about a special kind of relationship where participants give and receive honesty on demand. Of course, given human imperfection, this is easier said than done. Since we are all flawed, you and the others in your straight-talk relationship will need to cut one another slack.

Because people live dynamic lives, you'll find that your understanding of others and the situations they face requires continual updating. People change, their circumstances change, their needs and wants change. Keeping your straight-talk relationship intact requires investing energy to stay current. What's more, every relationship is different. You'll not only find your straight-talk partners unique but you'll discover a different *you* in each relationship. That's probably why you prize each relationship so strongly. While you may not have thought about it this way, that's part of the value and pleasure of having several straight-talk relationships. You get to experience several versions of yourself and you receive feedback and counsel from people who see you differently.

Communication between any two parties, even in the most stellar straight-talking relationship, is full of idiosyncratic biases, imperfections, and distortions. You may choose your words with care and precision, take pains to control facial expressions, and, to ensure accuracy, you may even e-mail one of your cohorts a summary of the thoughts you've spoken. But you should never count on the other person understanding your words and their meanings just as you intended them. All messages will be influenced by the recipient's ideas about your intent, their sensitivities about the topic, their personal history in trusting people in roles similar to yours, their views of your strengths and limitations, and every other variable you can think of, with the understanding that tomorrow more variables will be in play.

As I've been telling executives for years, "If you want to know what you said, you need to ask the other person what he or she heard."Once you get your answer, whether explicitly or by analyzing their response, you'll find yourself making adjustments that will allow the communication and the relationship to continue more fruitfully. You'll choose different words, use more or less stark phrases, use different examples, and find other strategies to make sure the other person interprets you correctly—that is, with the meaning you intended. Given all that is required to engage in straight-talk, you may be wondering if it is ever truly honest. It can be, albeit in degrees, and that's what I want to take up next. You need guidelines for expressing honesty, as well as criteria for judging the quality of honesty received.

> If you want to know what you said, you need to ask the other person what he or she heard.

In order to sort these out, consider the following hypothetical: you have a good friend—one with whom you talk straight—who frequently trims his bushy moustache on a right-to-left downward angle. This results in a noticeable gap between his moustache hair and lip on the right side and the moustache bristle overlapping his lip on the left. Your assignment: to tell him.

With one person you might bluntly say, "Do you realize your moustache is trimmed at an odd angle?" With another you might say, "This is probably my problem, but I'd like your mustache more if it were trimmed a little straighter." With a third person you might say, "I really like your moustache, always have, it's a very nice feature of your face and presentation. However, and I might be wrong about this, I think it's trimmed a bit crooked today. Look in the mirror, perhaps you can see what I mean." And with a fourth you might decide that this is not a topic he wants you commenting on and you'll leave it to someone else to tell him.

Many people would consider the first, blunt and factual statement, to be straight-talk and the next two something between excessive political correctness and bullsh*t. Many would consider the fourth option an abdication of responsibility. Some would call the second statement, featuring "I-speak," too safe and defensive for straight-talk. Some would see both the first and second as straight-talk and the as third bullsh*t because you, as speaker, are spending too much time building the person up prior to delivering a constructive criticism.

In my mind, any of the four could be straight-talk since the case could be made that each is relationship appropriate. In any straight-talk communication, you must assess the mind-set of the receiver and say what you think is necessary to keep the relationship viable. The moustache example may seem trivial but is actually a tricky communication since huge differences exist among people in their sensitivities to issues of physical appearances. Occasionally, you may have a straight-talk relationship that allows you to be bluntly honest on any topic you take up, but those are rare indeed. The vast majority require degrees of spin, subtlety, and tact. The question is where to draw the line between framing for accuracy of message and desired impact and framing primarily for agenda-related persuasion, aka *bullsh*t*.

I want to add another critical consideration to the aforementioned "it depends" answer about where to draw the line. It involves an analogy Jack McDonough and I wrote about in our book *Radical Management*. We drew a parallel between pocket billiards and trusting, straight-talk relationships.[1] In pocket billiards, you must consider two objectives simultaneously. You want to get balls in pockets and you want to leave the cue ball in a position to get more balls in pockets. So it is with relationships at work. There are always two objectives: getting your communication and influence across and maintaining the relationship in a way that allows future messages to get across, as you intend them to be heard.

Similarly, whatever topic is on the table right now, a straight-talk relationship requires awareness of the importance of maintaining the other person's goodwill in order to ensure your ability to hold the next candid, truth-as-one-knows-it communication. This includes recognition that unadorned candor used in the hope of getting immediate results can damage relationships. You must keep in mind that some honest communications may make the recipient unwilling to open themselves to your honesty again.

Mel, the CEO in the anecdote that opens this chapter, is one of my closest friends and most valued straight-talk cohorts. I wouldn't hesitate to tell him his moustache looked odd. Howard, on the other hand, has violated my trust in the past. I look for ways to build our relationship to facilitate future straight-talk. I would never put our tenuous relationship at risk by commenting on his facial hair!

At the macro-level, a straight-talk relationship considers three constituent entities—self, other, and others on the team (the team may include the company, professional discipline, or the system). At the micro-level, the third entity is the relationship itself. In other words, you need to consider the impact of any exchange on what the relationship can presently tolerate. And you want to prepare the way for increased candor in the future on topics that might be thought too sensitive to address today.

In judging whether an allegedly truthful communication constitutes "sufficient disclosure," I offer three elements to consider. The first was introduced in Chapter 4, and involves the timing and phrasing of what you say. Your honest statements should not make others excessively vulnerable or be injurious to their self-esteem. Second, you must take care not to bend or truncate what *you know* to the extent that an eventual full disclosure causes the recipient to believe that he or she was initially misled. The third element relates to your commitment to finding ways to eventually get beyond hedging and spinning to communicate more candidly the rest of the truth-*you*-know. Of course, what you're sharing has to overlap your cohort's desire to know it. That's a requirement for any straight-talk relationship. You must have the other person's agenda in focus, taking care to communicate your message in a format that allows that person to eventually accept a more complete version of it.

Everything I've written so far leads to the conclusion that most theories about exemplary human interactions are bunk. In communicating with others, you can't make "absolute truth," the criterion. Every human being is limited by the truth they can see, have known, and can tolerate. Even the justice system acknowledges this: you can't put someone in jail for not telling a better truth than that person believes. People with false beliefs about what has transpired can pass a polygraph test. In some ways, I wish I could restrict my definition of truth-telling to frank, direct, and simple statements of belief. But I can't. What's the use of stating a truth so bluntly that the recipient feels attacked, and thus can't hear it accurately? And you don't want to blurt out truths that you know will result in weakening a relationship, reducing the opportunity for future candor on topics of even greater importance.

Business roles, responsibilities, and protocol also need to be considered. It's often appropriate to keep confidences, for example, by not sharing information that's proprietary. Let's say you're the director of human resources and someone with whom you have a straight-talk relationship asks, "What's Ellen's salary?" You should have no problem saying, "It's improper for me to tell you." Of course, in practice people violate this ethic all the time. They cheat explicitly by revealing proprietary facts and they cheat indirectly with body and facial expressions such as shrugging their shoulders and rolling their eyes to communicate.

There are times when breaking protocol serves a valid organization purpose, as when someone "leaks" confidential information that people steering another department need to make an important decision more intelligently. This happens in corporate life, just as it does in government, where employees sometimes leak confidential reports to the press when they think normal checks and balances aren't working. Sometimes you feel you have to defy organization rules to make the system operate effectively. It's often said, "There are *no* secrets at work." I'd amend that by adding "outside of the confidences shared by people in straight-talk relationships." Confidences are broken all the time, especially in organizations that people find politically charged and where they perceive a lack of fair play. Although defying organizational protocol is often justified, the possibilities for mischief-making are many. That's one reason for my making "do no harm to others or the system" a defining feature of straight-talk relationships.

There are truths you withhold in order to protect your ability to communicate candidly in the future. There are truths you withhold because you believe nothing constructive will come from disclosing them. There are truths you withhold because of job responsibilities and company protocol. And there are truths you withhold in the service of furthering a self-interested agenda of your own. For example, what do you tell your significant other when asked, "Do you like the outfit I put together?" and the two of you are 15 minutes late leaving the house to meet another couple for dinner? Does a white-lie affirmative negate your entire straight-talk relationship? My ready answer for this: "It depends." In fact, that's always the correct answer, whatever the straight-talk relationship. You'll have to use your judgment, and that judgment requires attention to the three straight-talk criteria: active reflection of the truth-you-know, consideration of the other person's agenda and the sensitivities of the relationship, and the well-being of the broader team and system. When you withhold information, you must face the possibility that someone else in the relationship will interpret your withholding or bending the truth, as relationship betrayal, bullsh*t, or lying. You have to assess the likely risk/reward ratios of the actions you're considering.

Context is another critical consideration when framing a truth-you-know message in response to questions from your straight-talk cohort. Notice two variables are involved. There's the version of the truth-you-know that you think the other person should hear. And there's the truth the other person seeks, given his or her view of the situation. Neglecting either can have serious consequences. Each of us knows how upsetting it is to tell someone an essential truth that they cannot accept— especially one we thought would prevent a devastating setback for them. And many of us have had a falling out with a good friend because we didn't know how to honestly respond to a truth-seeking question we perceived as inappropriate.

To forestall such disappointments, I have a recommendation that I urge you to consider. It follows from everything else I've advised. The first words in any candid session that follows an explicit question from your straight-talk cohort should be, "How do you see it?" It's a question that will come naturally once you internalize the idea that everyone lives a different reality. This is at the core of the *Mind-Set Management* thesis.[2] Let me restate that principle. Resist telling someone a "truth" you think could hurt their feelings or negatively impact their self-esteem until you know their plan for using what you tell them.

No truth stands apart from context. Discovering someone's reason for asking and their plan for acting on what you tell them is relatively easy. All you have to do is ask yourself, "Why is this person asking for this truth now?" In other words, you need to tell yourself *a truth* prior to responding to a cohort's request to hear a truth. This strategy is so important that I take it up at length in Chapter 11.

The next section, Chapters 8–11, deals with the nitty-gritty practical issues of creating productive straight-talk relationships. These chapters will provide guidelines for overcoming obstacles to straight-talk and recognizing obstacles that can't be surmounted. One of the most important how-to's has already been introduced—the highly effective technique of "I-speak." Other skills and techniques for talking straight are described. And even when you choose not to reach out and talk straight, these chapters should leave you better equipped to spot bullsh*t when it comes your way—both your own and that of others.

APPLICATIONS SECTION

8
STRAIGHT-TALK
When Is It Possible with the Boss?

What happened is now company legend. Instantly everyone in the upper echelons heard the news. During a divisional overview it was slide number 101 that revealed a critical managerial blunder. In other words, 100 slides were shown prior to disclosing what top executives most essentially needed to know. The next day the floor opened up and swallowed that division's president. Within 24 hours there wasn't as much as a picture on her office wall.

Now management had an urgent problem. How to fill the vacated position? No time for an outside search, and, besides, a very viable candidate was already on the premises. This would be merely a one-step promotion for him. But to the bosses' surprise, the candidate didn't want it. His reasoning? "I'm perfectly happy in my present position," he explained. "I'm performing meaningful work and getting great recognition, earning more money than I ever imagined. Besides I plan to retire in a few years, and I have little interest in working frantically, cleaning up the mess that was left behind. Most of all, I don't want the pressure. I saw Georgia working 15–16 hours a day, 6 or 7 days a week. Who needs that?"

The bosses responded, "Take it; we'll help you. Wall Street is pressing for a seamless replacement. No question about you being the right person. No search could turn up someone more able. You have the credentials and reputation. You know the technology, you know the business. We'll make sure you succeed. There's no question about it, our skin is in this game. In retrospect we can see that we were partially responsible for Georgia's failure. We thought we could hold back on resources and push her to meet wish-list deadlines. Looks like we found out the hard way where that approach leads. We won't do anything like that with you. We'll give you the people slots you need, stop you when we think you're making unrealistic commitments, coach and guide you, give you a heads-up when something political is in the wind, and we'll make you rich beyond your dreams. You'll never have to conceal disappointing news because we know you're the absolute best. When problems arise we'll own them with you. Given our commitment it's hard to conceive of any program or project review requiring more than a dozen slides."

The outcome? Walt took the job, practices total disclosure with his bosses, is solicitous of ideas from below, works only a half day on weekends, and most days even has time to exercise. What's more, the bosses delivered on their promised support. They treat Walt respectfully and quickly get involved when there's a problem.

And what happened to the bosses? That part is disappointing. They failed to apply more widely what necessity had taught them to do. While they benefited from putting their "skin in the game" with Walt, they didn't use the same trust-building technique more broadly. To avoid repeats of what insiders now call "The Slide 101 Massacre," they had human resources institute a "deep dive" procedure in the other divisions reporting to them. This affords them a rationale for discussing operations with people reporting to division presidents they don't trust. They tell themselves that this way they get to hear it "all." Unfortunately the people they hear it from have no context for knowing what "all" needs telling. Face to face with a high-ranking executive asking penetrating questions, these managers behave as if they were taking a "test" to be promoted. They are prone to give answers that match their best guess of what the test-giver wants to hear.

EVERYONE YEARNS for a straight-talk relationship with their boss and, for that matter, with anyone in a position to do them some good. In fact, almost all job satisfaction surveys rank highest "a positive relationship with the boss." It's more important than pay, assignment, creative opportunities, or anything else. Of course, a positive relationship with the boss is one thing, a mentoring relationship is even better. A straight-talk relationship is an even greater step forward and, in my experience, far and away the rarest of these possibilities.

In any straight-talk relationship, especially one with a boss, both parties need to believe they have a *personal perspective* that the other truly values and wants to access. Keep in mind I said personal perspective, not technical expertise. I'm not talking about a CEO who needs a finance person who can be trusted or an advertising executive who needs a creative person clients like. I'm talking about subordinates and bosses who feel they have permission to comment on almost any matter bearing on the other's effectiveness and well-being.

When I reflect on boss-subordinate straight-talk relationships I've personally observed, I see that most were developed while the individuals were peers, prior to one being promoted to boss. Such relationships come with skill-set respect and established bonds of loyalty. I recall the Home Depot's cofounders, Bernard

Marcus and Arthur Blank, who were initially entrepreneurial partners. When I met them Bernie was CEO and Art was president. At the time they struck me as having a straight-talk relationship, candidly advising and coaching one another even though it was clear that Bernie was now Art's boss. It's also my experience that most one-time peers are less likely to talk straight once a direct chain-of-command relationship is established and a mandatory pay-and-performance review is involved.

The boss-subordinate relationship is a phenomenon I've been researching for years. It's a topic analyzed in detail in *Don't Kill the Bosses!* I began that research because I was puzzled about a common business situation that struck me as wacky. I asked myself, "Given all that's known about the benefits of teamwork, empowerment, and participatory decision making, how is it possible that, in the twenty-first century, we still have subordinates telling bosses what they think the boss wants to hear while bosses, who unabashedly blow smoke in their own bosses' eyes, walk around believing their subordinates have fully and honestly told them the truth as they know it?"

As I investigated, I found that all evidence pointed in one direction. Even though companies had everything to gain from subordinates telling it straight, corporate politics require bullsh*t. As to why, I discovered that people tend to be indiscriminate in their application and use of hierarchy. Most see no need to differentiate between hierarchical approaches to organizational *structure* and hierarchical approaches to *relationships*. But there's a big difference. Unambiguously designed, hierarchical structure, in the form of an organization chart, serves many constructive purposes. By showing the chain of command, it allows everyone to see who is responsible for what, how organization units are being deployed and, most importantly, who should be accountable for bottom line results. In contrast, I can't think of a single constructive purpose served by hierarchical relationships—that is, those in which the boss gets to dominate all conversations.

Unfortunately, most people with high positions in hierarchical structures have a twisted addiction to hierarchical relationships. Even when they don't wallow in having power over others, they like the efficiency that results from asserting their views without subordinate push-back. Even their idea of loyalty is warped. Despite solicitous words to the contrary, they don't act as if subordinate "loyalty" means "loyal enough to candidly assert what that person actually believes." They behave as if subordinate loyalty means "on-demand support and agreement" with their thinking. The classic statement of this view is movie mogul Samuel Goldwyn's much quoted remark, "I don't want any 'yes men' around me. I want everybody to tell me the truth, even if it costs them their jobs."

Don't Kill the Bosses! spells out the difference between hierarchical *structure* and hierarchical *relationships*. It points out the benefits of correctly designed hierarchical structure and criticizes the inevitable politics, dishonesty, and institutional corruption that result from hierarchy becoming a prominent feature of a boss-subordinate relationship. The book questions the practice of dismissing subordinates who fail to get results while allowing the bosses, who hired those subordinates and who are responsible for deploying, coaching, guiding, and overseeing them, to distance themselves from the train wrecks. Recall it was only a few months after the Abu Ghraib exposé that bosses on the scene of that America-damaging scandal were promoted and given Medals of Freedom. The corporals and privates who did what they thought they were supposed to do, albeit stupidly and self-indulgently, went to jail.

In *Don't Kill the Bosses!* I attribute the corruption in hierarchical relationships to one-sided accountability. In such relationships, only the bosses get to hold the subordinates accountable, and the bosses administer penalties at their discretion. As a healthier alternative, I prescribe two-sided accountability—relationships in which subordinates stand accountable for producing positive results and bosses stand accountable for giving the guidance and creating the conditions that allow subordinates to succeed. In this view, the bosses' number-one duty as leaders is choosing subordinates who have the capacity to contribute to the organization and providing the tools and conditions for their success. It's interesting to note that hardly any boss invokes the word *accountability* when what he or she wants has been produced. The word *accountability* is reserved for times when bosses fail to get the performances and outcomes they desire.

Within the framework of the *Beyond Bullsh*t* book you're now reading, only one word is relevant to creating accountability. That word is *consequences*. Without consequences any action taken to produce accountability is essentially meaningless, because the only purpose actually served is persuading onlookers that appropriate action has been taken. But what's *appropriate action* if nothing tangible results from taking it?

Unfortunately, when most people think consequences they think *punishment*. This is particularly regrettable because fear of punishment is the chief obstacle to people owning up to the problems they cause. Who admits error in the face of out-of-proportion punishment for owning up? When stopped for speeding how many people tell the officer the truth if they can invent an excuse that might spare them a citation? And when stopped, how many go on to explain with integrity, "Officer, perhaps I was speeding but it was because I was in a hurry to get home from an office celebration where the drinking got a little out of hand."

There's another word related to consequences that people rarely consider outside of a straight-talk relationship. That word is *learning*. Within a straight-talk relationship, the consequence of a failed performance should be personal development, new perspective, improved judgment, skill enhancement, and general all-around learning. If the cohort is one's boss, so much the better. In a straight-talk relationship, both have the opportunity to learn. Subordinates learn what they need to do differently to achieve desired results, and bosses learn what type of support and guidance the subordinate needed but did not receive. Then both can look forward to what must be done in the future to achieve a better outcome.

In the two-sided accountability model, if the subordinate flubbed, the boss flubbed. Moreover, if it's determined that the needed lessons are outside the boss's ability to teach them, then it's time to break up that reporting relationship. Either get a new boss for the subordinate or free the subordinate to look for a job where success is possible. But don't pin a Medal of Freedom or a fourth unwarranted star on a boss who failed in training subordinates to succeed and dodged responsibility for their failed performance.[1] That boss flubbed his assignment.

In the anecdote that opens this chapter, the bosses learned the valuable "skin in the game" lesson that allowed them to fill a managerial gap with an initially reluctant candidate. However, when they failed to apply that lesson more generally, everyone in the company lost out. And it wasn't just any lesson. These guys let the two-way accountability "grail" slip through their fingers! "Skin in the game" commitment to the other person's success and well-being is a requirement for any straight-talk relationship. And it's an essential but missing dimension in most boss-subordinate relationships.

In a straight-talk relationship each person must feel secure with the other, and that's never more true than when status differences are involved. This entails each person believing he or she has personal perspectives, traits, and vantage points that the other person should and does value. Those qualities might be almost anything—industry experience, intellectual prowess, emotional maturity, problem solving under pressure, people skills, even wealth or spirituality. They are often qualities that the other cohort sees as complementary, and this contributes to the sense that it's a relationship of equals. Whatever the qualities, I'm talking about a relationship in which each person feels they can say a good deal of what they think without fear of punishment or rejection.

Subordinates who think telling truths the boss doesn't want to hear will negatively affect their performance ratings don't talk straight to their bosses. Of course, this doesn't rule out candid topical conversations, daily camaraderie, and genuinely warm and supportive interactions. But there's little chance such interactions will morph into straight-talk relationships as long as issues involving pay, assignment, and career progress loom in the background. Parenthetically, this is why most high-level executives go without formal performance reviews. Unlike their underlings, they are merely told each year about adjustments in pay and bonuses, with few if any specific references to how their performance has actually been evaluated. Basically, the only personal feedback they receive is that they get to keep their jobs. The lack of executive reviews is prima facie evidence of the difficulty of maintaining straight-talk relationships between those who give performance reviews and those who receive them. This problem would disappear if pay and evaluation systems were changed to be less screwy. I've addressed this topic before in the book *Mind-Set Management*.[2] Some of what I wrote pertains to what I'm discussing now.

Mind-Set Management argues that standard pay and performance review practices are illogical on two fronts—first, for conducting pay and performance reviews in a single meeting and, second, for conducting them at all. Regretfully, this remains common practice. Even more egregious is the fact that these reviews are now often billed—incorrectly—as two-way give-and-take exchange. But most subordinates sense immediately that this is a boss-constructed and boss-serving pretense. Whatever the bosses say, they usually had their minds made up about performance and pay long before the alleged give-and-take session takes place. And when subordinates try to correct what they see as mistaken judgments about them, they often find their bosses have deaf ears.

> Standard pay and performance review practices are illogical on two fronts—first, for conducting pay and performance reviews in a single meeting and, second, for conducting them at all.

When pay and performance reviews are combined, subordinates face a political nightmare. Even as they are trying to show that they deserve an evaluation that merits additional pay, their bosses are calling for performance changes using examples that illustrate improvement is needed. Obviously it is self-defeating for the subordinate to agree. Moreover, in most cases, the subordinates don't think their boss has their strengths and contributions in clear enough focus. In fact, when it comes to performance reviews, it is only when a close friend is doing the evaluation that most subordinates feel that their contributions are being evaluated accurately, using appropriate criteria and metrics. Adding to the unpleasantness, most subordinates sense that standing up for the truth-as-they-know-it will only make things worse. It's not that subordinates don't recognize that they have flaws. Rather, they fear that resisting their boss's "truth" will be read as "defensiveness," adding one more deficiency to the boss's list of "improvements needed."

Although subordinates may not realize it, the boss faces a political dilemma of his or her own that further complicates the whole unholy process. Even if the subordinate were able to convince the direct-line boss of his or her competence and worthiness, the boss would have to sell this new perspective upward to the next-level boss, the person who probably weighed the initial opinions and decided on the size of the raise. The direct-line boss now is faced with confronting the next-level boss and saying something like, "Roger convinced me his deficiencies aren't what we thought. I now believe he is right and deserves more pay than was initially budgeted for him." Good luck to the middle manager who takes that tack when the time comes for his or her "wimpy" performance to be reviewed.[3]

Contributing to the painful illogic of the process is the cultural pretense that pay and performance are connected. This pretense usually surfaces only after the initial hiring. At hiring, the disconnect is obvious. Compensation is determined before the individual performs even one day's work. Sometimes there's a little show of acting as if the two are related, such as when initial compensation is broken into a predetermined salary plus a bonus "contingent" on meeting preestablished expectations for performance. But, more often than not, first-year bonuses are sure things, and when results are disappointing, shortfalls are readily forgiven. Why? Because despite corporate pretense to the contrary, the initial compensation package was primarily determined by marketplace considerations.

Wackiness returns to the process at the time of the first pay and performance review. That's when company protocol instructs the boss to link pay to performance. But such thinking doesn't change the basic fact: pay is marketplace driven and has little enduring effect on the quality of performance. Bonuses or implied threats may be used to extract more hours and intensification of effort, but even such incentives and threats seldom have long-term impact. Don't forget, people's egos and self-esteem are involved. As long as pay is competitive, most people will knock themselves out trying to perform their best and to please their bosses.

Looked at this way, standardized performance metrics are red herrings used mostly to intimidate and control. No matter what the bosses write in the performance review, if the second year's raise isn't sufficient, the subordinate may pick up and go somewhere else. Of course, whether the person leaves depends on "somewhere else" paying materially more once transaction costs and future opportunities are factored in. The present bosses too must weigh the real cost of the transaction since there are costs to losing a person with known skills and hiring a replacement with hearsay talents and yet-to-be-discovered limitations.

In my view, lumping pay and performance reviews together is little more than disorienting corporate theatre. It is a demoralizing annual rite that produces vast amounts of bullsh*t that tend to undermine boss-subordinate straight-talk relationships that would serve the organization, and the individuals, far better. Straight-talk requires a paradigm shift in which compensation is recognized as the marketplace-dependent variable it is and performance is linked to boss/subordinate chemistry. How might this work?

First, bosses need to decide what kind of raises and other forms of compensation they are willing to offer. Part of that decision involves self-assessment. Bosses need to analyze their comfort level with the subordinate, their beliefs about the subordinate's talent and skills, and their beliefs about their own capacity to provide what is necessary to maximize the subordinate's productivity. The bosses also need to assess subordinate expectations and make a judgment about how he or she values the current compensation package. Finally, bosses need to study the marketplace. They need to know what people in comparable roles receive and estimate the availability of replacement personnel. Once the compensation package is determined, it should be communicated to the subordinate impersonally—perhaps written down and handed to the subordinate in a sealed envelope.

At this point it's up to the subordinate either to agree or to negotiate. If the choice is to negotiate, the ensuing "conversation" should be exclusively about pay. Care should be taken by both sides not to discuss performance quality or perceived "faults." If the boss doesn't like the quality of the subordinate's performance and can get someone more to his or her liking, the boss should do so. But it serves no constructive purpose for the boss to attack a subordinate's self-concept or to argue that the subordinate lacks the skills required for better performance. Those discussions should be reserved for another day.[4]

In the model I advocate, bosses can talk performance, skill development, and quality of effort any other day of the year. In fact they can make it a daily activity once it's clear that the subordinates know that the boss is committed to their success and well-being. It is only when pay is the topic that such conversations should be avoided. Pay has to do with functions performed and how the boss values the subordinate's way of performing them. A boss who feels a subordinate is not yet performing an entire function should avoid suggesting that the company can't pay X for only half a function performed. If the company can find someone to perform the entire job and wants to pay the transition costs, the company should hire that alternative person immediately. Otherwise bosses should keep the grousing to themselves. If a boss needs to change a person's job, they should do so. But a boss should not use need-for-improvement as a negotiating tool for limiting pay. Doing so will only breed resentment. It is unlikely that either the boss or the subordinate will convince the other their views are "objective," let alone intrinsically valid. An adversarial discussion on such a highly charged and political topic is pointless. Don't destroy goodwill in a relationship that most participants want to see as reciprocally supportive.

The *Don't Kill the Bosses!*[5] concept of two-sided, boss and subordinate accountability makes clear that any one-party performance *review* is pointless. If it's a *review*, then it should be a review of what the boss and subordinate accomplished or did not accomplish, working together as an entity. This requires sincere *I-speak* and *we-speak*, never "you did or didn't" allegations. Results obtained by the subordinate should not be separated from the supports provided by the boss. Don't forget, the boss played a critical role in staging the conditions that yielded last year's performance and results. When it comes to getting work done the boss-subordinate team is the responsible and accountable party.

In this context, candor requires self-critique and self-honesty, not finger-pointing on the part of the boss in response to unrealized expectations. No after-the-fact, one-sided review of a subordinate is going to change last year's numbers. The company benefits far more when the conversation is focused on next year's bottom line. What's more, the conversation is likely to be far more candid when the focus is on how are we going to accomplish this together, rather than haggling about what the subordinate did or failed to do. Thus, the format I recommend is a performance *pre*view discussing what *we* are going to do together. This is the far more productive alternative to conventional relationship-weakening, *you*-focused, performance *re*views. Applying the two-sided accountability model makes performance *re*views obsolete.

Practically speaking, performance *pre*views ought to facilitate candid discussions about effectiveness, particularly if both the boss and subordinate use I-speak. There are no buried bodies to account for, no alleged mistakes to explain away, and little reason to assign blame. This is one of those times when people can maximize candor and rational discussion. Bosses and subordinates exchange views on what they individually think needs to be "*we*-achieved." They discuss what results constitute valid measures of interim progress and the likelihood of their jointly reaching commonly held goals. Then the boss and subordinate can candidly discuss resource requirements, actions to be taken and what type of involvement and personal commitment each is able to give. It's in this context, prior to problems occurring, that the boss and subordinate can be up front stating what they need from one another, what part of that has been missing, how others in the company view what they're doing, and what more may be needed in the way of resources, skills, coaching, oversight, and the involvement of others in the company.

Whatever's decided should lead to periodic, even daily, "checking-in" discussions. Questions to be asked might include "How do you see the situation?" "How do you see me performing?" "What do you need from me?" and "What do you hear me asking for that you don't know how to do?" Communicating frequently becomes part of the process in which the boss and subordinate team up to produce results both desire. Because the boss has skin in the game, his or her oversight becomes as natural as someone calling home on their way out the office door to ask, "Honey, is there anything you'd like me to pick up on my way home?" Just as the caller realizes it's his or her dinner too, those in successful boss-subordinate straight-talk relationships understand that their common good is at stake.

Changing the system to embrace two-sided accountability and performance previewing goes a long way toward setting the stage for boss-subordinate straight-talk relationships. Also required, however, is the ability to face up to differences and to negotiate conflicts. This ability is all but lost in prototypical one-sided accountability relationships where bosses dominate. That's why, regardless of positive intent, combined pay and performance review sessions quickly revert to bullsh*t spoken and received. In this new, improved paradigm, the question for each party becomes "What do you need from me to get the results we desire?"

In the end, it's interpersonal chemistry, trust, and loyalty that determine the level of candor possible in a boss-subordinate relationship. The probabilities of candor leading to straight-talk increase when pay and performance are separated. The probabilities increase further when "we-*previews*," not "you-*reviews*," are the means for encouraging good performance. And the odds improve even further when boss and subordinates discuss their differences using I-speak. Whatever the setting, candor depends on cohorts accepting that differences in view-point and interpretation of events are inevitable, whether or not they are evident at the time.

9

STRAIGHT-TALK
Benefits/Liabilities

Magic theatre. Entrance not for everybody.
—Hermann Hesse, *Steppenwolf*

It took one weird handshake to illustrate what can be learned as a result of a matter-of-fact, straight-talk question. The handshake was given by a 45-year-old Oklahoma City-raised and -based manager I had just met. A quick-to-the-draw gripper, his handshake determined what I was able to do in response. The back of his hand cupped outward so that there was no way for our palms to touch. What he did struck me as so odd that I asked for a second handshake. This time I tried to shake his hand my way but again he was too fast. I wanted our palms to touch but that was impossible shaking hands his way. I asked, "Where did you learn to shake hands like that?" He answered, "Like what?" I said, "Well it's a distinctive handshake, one that keeps our palms from touching." He replied, "Everyone shakes hands like that." I started laughing and said, "Of course, everyone shakes your hand that way. You're such a fast gripper, no one has an alternative." He said, "All the men in my family shake hands that way." Still laughing I replied, "If they're as fast as you, I bet all their friends shake hands that way, too." We both laughed.

Then I asked for a chance to grip first, to show him the palm-touching alternative. I said, "That's how I usually shake hands and, I think, most people do as well. Watch them." Later on he told me the exchange had caused him to wonder what else others could tell him about how he thinks and acts. I thought, "Point, set, match."

UP, DOWN, SIDEWAYS, and diagonally, you'll find straight-talk relationships essential to your success at work. No other form of communication produces comparable benefits. And you'll reap the benefits of straight-talk immediately once you acknowledge a much ignored fact: *at work, few interactions are disposable.* Conversations that appear incidental and inconsequential, with time, can become monumentally important. You need straight-talking cohorts to keep you current on what you may miss.

Star billing on the list of benefits is straight-talk providing you a reality check. Straight-talk relationships can be used as sounding boards for actions you're uncertain about. They are sources of feedback for measuring your impact, by people whose responses you can usually trust. You get the reflections of individuals who by temperament and inclination proceed differently from you—and such diversity of views is a proven basis for making better decisions. Straight-talk cohorts cheer for you to succeed and usually will tell you what they feel in their hearts. While they may not always understand what you are doing or why, they are open to finding out. And when something in your relationship with third parties is "off," you can usually count on them noticing and providing instant advice.

Notwithstanding the objectivity and truthfulness intended and professed by your cohorts, it's important to keep what they tell you in perspective. All you're getting in the way of feedback and reality checks is I-speak. Never expect others to tell you the

> Never expect others to tell you the absolute truth; they don't have it to give.

absolute truth; they don't have it to give. All that's possible is the truth-they-know, given their knowledge of you, the situation, and their own self-interests and personal biases. Naturally it follows that the more your straight-talk cohorts know about you and your self-interested pursuits, the better assistance they can render. Nevertheless, extrapolating from a cohort's view of say, how another colleague regards you, is a judgment you'll have to make.

Inevitably your feelings and thoughts about a straight-talk cohort will affect what you hear in their messages. You'll construe the meaning of words spoken and actions taken by Person A differently than you would construe the same words and actions from Person B. When it comes to extracting meaning from a cohort's feedback, your history with the other person, your beliefs about their mind-sets, and the work and life situations you see them living will impact your interpretation of everything you see and hear.

Straight-talk relationships provide a ready means for inquiring into the logic, thinking, and realities that led your cohort to take actions that make little sense to you. This is especially useful in a business relationship where people think differently using intelligence that escapes your reasoning. A straight-talk relationship gives you permission to matter-of-factly raise questions that you might not otherwise ask for fear of having them perceived as naive, critical, or socially improper. In straight-talk relationships, you don't have to guess people's reactions and thinking. You are free to bluntly ask: "What's your reasoning, I came out differently?" "You look bothered. Is it something I said?" "What are you going to say to the marketing guy?" "What's your real problem with Finance?" "What's your best guess about the reactions we're going to get?" "What's your conclusion?" You don't have to leave a meeting guessing. You can ask point-blank and trust the integrity of the response you get. More often than not what you hear is going to be surprising. When people talk straight, far more idiosyncratic complexity—invaluable complexity—is revealed than in the more typical beating-around-the-bush exchange of bullsh*t.

Straight-talk relationships have an efficiency everyone finds attractive. Operating with minimal need to hide self-interests allows you to get quickly to the point. You need three minutes, not four hours, to cover a three-minute topic. You get to the crux of matters while there's still time to act. Without straight-talk you're stuck using bullsh*t, formulated and packaged to be persuasive with others responding in kind. But messages sent and received with bullsh*t seldom prove convincing or useful. Straight-talk allows you to ask questions that elicit answers you'll trust enough to act on.

A straight-talk relationship is a vehicle for harmonizing agendas with people you would like as organizational allies. Such a relationship is an opportunity for learning about a cohort's commitments and the obstacles they face in supporting agendas important to you. In straight-talk relationships, cohorts share certain assumptions that usually keep them on the same track. However, you don't want to burden an otherwise positive relationship by asking for support on a matter that others can't deliver while staying true to themselves. On the other hand, you shouldn't presume you know how a cohort thinks until you have inquired. But caution should always be exercised when asking. Once you inquire about someone's views and that person responds, he or she will think you've got their message straight. And if you don't declare to the contrary, their inclination is to assume you have agreed. Having "heard" you agree, others will feel betrayed if you subsequently act differently than they expected you to behave.

Straight-talk relationships generate a positive spirit that helps reconcile disparities in the agendas of you and your cohorts. More often than not, there will be a mutual desire to revise and realign so that differences reconcile without relationship-disrupting conflict. Especially in large companies, you need people who are aligned with your needs to help you negotiate politicized issues that hamper your progress. You need people looking out for your interests when you aren't in the room to protect them. Because straight-talk relationships produce loyalty and because further loyalty is forged in the process of aligning agendas, straight-talk cohorts are likely to see supporting what's important to you as consonant with their own self-interested pursuits.

Straight-talk cohorts play a valuable role in keeping you posted on organizational happenings and interpreting those events. Cohorts often have insights about issues you find perplexing. They are vital second-opinion resources in gauging your relationships with third parties. They help you identify issues and sensitivities you overlooked. No doubt you already have reliable ways of tracking your organizational concerns. Cohorts provide additional avenues and may contribute skills to your repertoire that you lack. It's not that cohorts are without myopia and bias. But their limitations are different from yours, and their skills and insights are often complementary.

Straight-talk relationships offer a ready means for freely verbalizing your preliminary reactions to organizational events and for getting another person's ideas on how to present your agendas persuasively. Cohorts can preview your plan, critique your request for resources, help you explain why your project was delayed, and help you justify a raise. They can even give advice on how to conduct your office politics more effectively.

Elsewhere I have written: *"politics are; all that needs to be determined is how they're going to be conducted."*[1] Politics are the natural consequence of people vying to frame and structure organizational events to conform to their self-interested pursuits. Because everyone has different self-interests, politics are an omnipresent challenge. Straight-talk cohorts provide ready access and vital advice for managing your image, asserting your authority, designing projects, and maintaining daily credibility—all important facets of succeeding at corporate politics.

Most of the time you'll find that straight-talk creates an enduring interpersonal connection. It produces bonds of loyalty that exceed the value of any specific discussion. As a result, straight-talk relationships provide you with a power-taking advantage. Confident that your cohort will go along with what you think, you can state your views with clarity and integrity. You have a good sense of the backing you'll receive and what not to say that could erode it. Your cohorts' support gives you the confidence to tell third parties what you honestly think, to assert your expertise and authority in a meeting, and to hold your ground without excessive mealymouthing when others resist your thinking.

WHEN STRAIGHT-TALK IS NOT ADVISED

Notwithstanding straight-talk's potential benefits, you need to be cautious when considering a straight-talk relationship. You should not indulge in straight-talk impulsively in response to a pressing need of the moment. While straight-talk begets straight-talk, it doesn't trump organizational politics, human defensiveness, different capacities for straight-talk, the dynamics of the present situation, or relationship rifts from the past. You need to pick your cohorts carefully.

Straight-talk is only recommended with people who have the capacity and inclination to follow through and reciprocate. In many ways this is the mirror image of what is required of you. You need to ask yourself: Does a prospective cohort have the desire to self-reflect with a level of honesty that's acceptable to me? Does this person have the ability to focus on agendas related to my success while struggling with his or her own? Does this person seem to be basically constructive, observing ethics and eschewing tactics that exploit others? Does this person find me attractive enough for purposes of friendship and sociability?

You'll be most vulnerable in straight-talk relationships when they reveal the biases that underlie your responses to organizational events. These personal patterns become apparent as cohorts search to account for variances between the truths you relate and the alternative truths they believe. As your unique mind-sets and orientations become clear, your friends will be inclined to call them sensitivities and strong suits and talk about your personal attributes with respect. But people who aren't so friendly will call the same qualities liabilities. They will self-servingly trivialize your unique strengths and contributions and refer to them in ways third parties will find negative. What your friends describe as your "ability to work well with others," your non-friends may call "sucking up" and "conflict averse." Of course, straight-talk relationships will reveal some limitations that even you might characterize as "shortcomings." But you and your friends will tend to place these limitations in a context that shows them to be inconsequential compared to your possessing strengths and proficiencies that many others lack.

At this point you may be thinking, "Why plunge all at once into straight-talk?" You think you might be able to initiate straight-talk on a low-risk topic and then quickly pull back without much vulnerability if the other person fails to respond in kind. Probably you can. But keep in mind that you'll lose the "pullback option" once the other person jumps in with straight-talk of their own. More quickly than you might have imagined, questions will be asked, you'll respond, and candor will have spread to topics you never anticipated.

Whether straight-talk will work for or against you depends as much on the agendas you pursue as your chemistry with the other person. Once again you must ask yourself questions. Is the other person saying and doing what they think you want to hear in order to entice you into a temporary alliance? If you decide they are, don't assume they realize it—people are often taken in by their own sincerity. Only after a solid relationship has been established will you have a platform strong enough to withstand occasional lapses in authenticity. Hence a conundrum: Straight-talk breeds trust, support, friendship, and loyalty, but you don't want to talk straight with people until your relationship already has those qualities.

The easiest and least risky time for straight-talk is when someone else initiates it. Then the other person's outreach is evidence of their desire for a straight-talk relationship. Your vulnerability is hedged. But you still need to decide if you can trust their reaching out and whether responding in kind serves your interests.

When you believe another party is not up for a straight-talk relationship, you're foolish to proceed without bullsh*t. Your reasons for deciding against straight-talk will vary. It may be the other person's inability to keep a confidence; it may be your belief that they lack the desire or ability to form an enduring bond. Whatever the source of your reluctance, you'll have to use judgment. You also have to assess your own record in reading other people. Think about the false positives, the people you trusted that you shouldn't have; and the false negatives, the people you failed to trust who turned out to be extremely worthy. The good news here is that many people have far more capacity for straight-talk than they initially exhibit and that most relationships take some time to jell. In my experience, most people who initially appear aloof and defensive actually value and seek friendship, candor, and intimacy but lack sophistication initiating it.

A straight-talk relationship is a precarious path to start down if later you find yourself needing to backtrack. Of course, intuition, situational imperatives, emotions of the moment, even chance, will play important, even overriding, roles in deciding whether to initiate a straight-talk relationship and how much to open up in response to another person's openness. The next chapter deals with assessing your own and a potential cohort's capacities for straight-talk.

10

STRAIGHT-TALK
Conditions for Getting It

Sir Geoffrey Vickers once drew a powerful analogy based on a narrow trap that could catch a lobster but not a crab, which could back up and spin around: "A trap is a trap only for creatures which cannot solve the problems that it sets. Man-traps are dangerous only in relation to the limitations on what men can see and value and do. The nature of the trap is a function of the nature of the trapped. To describe either is to imply the other."[1]

Likewise, I believe each person is able to see and value and do some things others cannot, and, at the same time, misses seeing, valuing, and doing what others, with different abilities, do readily. Unlike lobsters, we have the resources to avoid getting trapped. One of the best is our straight-talk relationships.

I'VE LOOKED AT STRAIGHT-TALK from many angles, but, in the end, I remain convinced that each participant should embrace the three Chapter 5–mentioned conditions when entering such a relationship. There must be a commitment to telling the truth one knows and being other-sensitive when telling it. There must be a commitment to getting the agendas of one's straight-talk cohorts in focus and looking out for their interests along with your own. And there needs to be shared concern for conducting self-interested pursuits in an ethical, moral and non-harmful way with respect to others on the team: work group, company, marketplace, and system. Unless each of these conditions is met, the ensuing conversations and actions are likely to end in disappointment and eventually in resentment as glitches, inevitable in all relationships, arise.

Straight-talk relationships emerge naturally when people like each other, respect each other's competence, know each other's situation, accept each other's limitations and sensitivities, recognize one another's interests, and refrain from any bum-rapping. In other words, a straight-talk relationship is natural between people committed to supporting one another's quests for success and well-being.

The most common place to find straight-talk is in established relationships, with people you know well and have good reason to judge trustworthy and loyal. These may be former school-mates, people with whom you worked closely in the past, those with whom you've exchanged kindnesses, or people who have seen you both at your best and your worst, perhaps those with whom you've shared a major success or disappointment. You would be surprised and upset if such people failed to communicate with you in a forthright, above-board manner. You'd be equally surprised if they had taken an action without concern for your well-being or had failed to counter someone who disparaged your accomplishments or overemphasized your faults. These are also people who would always try to intervene if they thought you were about to do or say something ill advised.

Another pool from which to draw straight-talk cohorts is work associates who do not see themselves as pitted in win-lose, zero-sum competition with you. These could be people in your own work unit. More likely they're people working in different units, in roles not linked to yours on an organization chart, even people working in different companies who can imagine you joining them in a mutually beneficial alliance. Potential cohorts may seek political support in a particular situation or personal support in order to improve their overall effectiveness and affirm and reexamine important life assumptions. Both motives involve compelling self-interests, but the latter, involving self-reflection is usually more conducive to straight-talk.

New acquaintances also present opportunities for straight-talk relationships, but, again, only when their political interests align with yours. New relationships afford minimum-baggage occasions to strike up friendships, share confidences, and offer organizational intelligence and personal advice. It's minimum baggage, not no baggage, because everyone brings personal baggage along. You can't leave home without it. Some of that baggage dates back to sensitivities developed when growing up in one's nuclear family, some to subsequent experiences, and some to troublesome issues raised by a current situation.

For example, consider an e-mail exchange I had with a student holding a very responsible job enrolled in our MBA program for the fully employed. Sensing self-defeating baggage, I instinctively started probing. Fortunately, my "sent mail" folder kept a record of a lesson she found "enormously useful." Here's what we exchanged.

STUDENT: Hi Professor, I am frantically trying to fax you the paper but it appears your fax is not on. Separately I have e-mailed you the paper with an explanation as to its lateness. Thanks

PROF: Why are you frantic? What have I ever done to raise your anxieties about a "late" paper? What's the purpose of the time boundary? I could read your paper 30 min before class. Pls don't sweat it. I'm glad to print your e-mail. I think the fax in my office IS turned off. Why ARE you frantic? Is this related to your past?

STUDENT: Thanks Professor! Yes I was frantic. This is something I do know about myself. If I have a deadline, project due, or anything else that I know people are relying or expecting me to meet then I panic if I feel I am not doing it. I want you to know that you CAN rely on me.

PROF: Why would I doubt it?

Given that everyone comes with baggage, you'll find straight-talk relationships providing you and your cohorts many opportunities to put handles on luggage that the other person would like to control. When people trust you, they don't take offense when you helpfully comment, "your slip is showing" or "your shirt is out in the back."

You'll find *commiseration* is another common basis for forming straight-talk relationships, notwithstanding that it's less than ideal. The impetus is often mutually perceived unfairness and a shared sense of injustice. Cohorts may share feelings of vulnerability or a sense of being institutionally one-down. The basis for these feelings might be a discriminatory company practice, problems with a common boss, low status or a meaningless assignment, insufficient resources to perform well, the presence of a glass ceiling, or some other situation where cohorts bond for support in a world they experience as unfair.

Relationships born of commiseration require careful monitoring to ensure they develop the constructiveness that straight-talk requires. At work it is commonplace for people to operate with dual sets of ethics. There's high-minded morality, normally exhibited prior to someone feeling unfairly treated, victimized by dirty tactics, being lied to or manipulated, or having the system stacked against them. In contrast, there's the no-holds barred, street fighter, dog-eat-dog ethic people often adopt once they feel they've been "screwed." The constant challenge for straight-talk relationships is to find a way to drop the negative feelings and chip-on-the-shoulder cynicism and to restore positive feelings and high-minded ethics as soon as possible. In the end, cohorts must shun collusion and conspiracy. If they fail to develop constructive intent, they may collude in directing toward others the same sort of double-dealing they so resented when it was directed their way.

A shared, non-mainstream common identity is another impetus for straight-talk relationships. The driving force can be almost any commonality—same faith, ethnicity, temperament, favorite football team, social class, high school, family, or chiropractor. It's strange how almost any common characteristic or shared experience can lead to feelings of interpersonal attraction, affiliation, and trust.

WHAT A STRAIGHT-TALK RELATIONSHIP REQUIRES FROM YOU

Regardless of how intellectually and emotionally attractive you find someone, or the urgency of your need for support, you should have your personal house in order prior to beginning a straight-talk relationship. To do so, you have to minimize the human penchant to bullsh*t yourself. This entails making a real effort to uncover the personal biases and idiosyncratic mind-sets that color your views of people and events. You'll find valuable clues to these biases and mind-sets in some of the feedback you receive, particularly if you have the courage to treat all feedback, however harsh, as valuable information. Doing so requires paying particular attention to what you don't at all want to hear. Of course, awareness of what others think doesn't mean you have to change anything, although you might do yourself a great favor by doing so. It merely requires acknowledging that parts of the organizational world you inhabit are

> Parts of the organizational world you inhabit are of your own making and it's in your best interest to discover what those elements are.

of your own making and it's in your best interest to discover what those elements are.

People are more likely to level with you when they think you're sincere in your efforts to self-improve. Others will respond positively if they sense that you genuinely desire greater understanding of self and the situation you are in, better interactions with others, and upgraded skill levels in relationships. They will respond to your willingness to learn by telling you things they think you should know. People will be energized by your openness to their views. On the other hand, enthusiasm for a straight-talk relationship dims when cohorts see you acting closed off and defensive. Nobody expects you to drop all your defenses—they wouldn't either. But other people will appreciate your willingness to minimize knee-jerk self-protection and carefully listen to what they find important enough to say. By definition, straight-talk relationships are coalitions between people with different viewpoints. Such relationships contrast sharply with political coalitions, which depend on shared viewpoints. The goals of straight-talk relationships are also different. Such relationships strive for more than the success of a shared political platform; they strive for increased consciousness leading to greater personal effectiveness and life success for each individual.

When you demonstrate open-mindedness, cohorts are emboldened to raise sensitive topics and to engage in robust, give-and-take, candid, thoughtful discussions that can provide you with invaluable insight. At the end of the day, straight-talk cohorts expect you to step outside your "box" to confront what they fear you haven't perceived correctly. I once published a pamphlet entitled "The Interpersonal Process of Self-Disclosure: It Takes Two to See One."[2] After years of research, I think that title is more on the money than ever.

As one psychology experiment after another has demonstrated, it's human nature to exaggerate adulation and downplay criticisms. Doing so bolsters self-esteem. It's also human nature to go through periods of self-doubt, when self-perceived flaws loom exaggeratedly large. We are also under social pressure to present a modest, can-do, positive façade and to conceal any swings in self-esteem. As a result, sometimes we have to dig to determine our own reality and concentrate hard to not distort how we present ourselves to others. Straight-talk relationships require self-authenticity, first and foremost. Next, they require the courage to confide the truths we believe as candidly as we might deem prudent in the moment.

Straight-talk relationships require a very different style of communication than you get with bullsh*t. In straight-talk, you have to curtail the self-promotional and limit the self-ingratiating. No straight-talk cohort wants to see you be disingenuous or hear you use braggadocio with the purpose of image management. And no straight-talk cohort wants to hear you begin a sentence with "To be quite honest with you . . . ," implying you haven't been honest up until now. No straight-talk cohort wants to see you act sincere and friendly when seeking favors from people they know you disdain. No straight-talk cohort wants to hear you talk of sacrificing for the good of others and the company when they know the biggest winner will be you. No straight-talk cohort wants to hear you say that you're speaking objectively and doing what the organization truly needs when they know that self-interests are your primary drivers (and theirs). These are the conventions of bullsh*t, not straight-talk.

For all the virtues of straight-talk relationships, there are times when they prove quite difficult. You may be exasperated when straight-talk cohorts expect you to greet their every comment with an open mind. You may silently bristle when they tactlessly criticize actions you've already taken and can't reverse. They'll frustrate you arguing business points that counter what you've done or committed. There will be moments when their critiques put you on the defensive. They may make blunt comments about your friends that you find offensive, even slanderous. You won't like it when they dismiss some contribution you've made as inconsequential that you thought was importantly valuable. There will be times when cohorts criticize you without having their facts straight or say things that sound more about them than about you. In the face of all this, how do you keep your personal equilibrium? How do you separate what rings true from what misses the mark, knowing that others stop telling it straight when they experience you as defensive?

Your ability to respond with an open mind will be challenged every time you hear accounts of events that differ significantly from how you perceived them. When cohorts tread on sensitive areas and misread you, you probably won't think to say something disarming, such as: "Please go easy. I'm extremely sensitive here." Instead you're likely to react like any normal person—with emotion, even anger. Staying open-minded is always a challenge on topics where your need for control causes you to want the last word. But commitment to straight-talk means accepting that you won't always have control, won't always be able to manage your image, and having the "last word" may not happen any time this year.

Straight-talk also demands that you remain mindful that, in life and especially at work, motivation and personal history drive perception and that, bias and distortion notwithstanding, your cohort's perception is their reality. This fact of human nature has been expressed in many ways: "Where one stands determines what one sees," "It's all about mind-sets," "People view life through unique filters," "The organization is an artifact of the mind that views it," "Life is *Rashomon*," and others. A classic psychology experiment from the 1940s established the universality of this phenomenon. Schoolchildren were asked to draw pictures of coins projected on a screen. The children from what we now call "economically challenged" backgrounds drew their coins significantly larger than those from "economically privileged" homes.

GETTING THE OTHER PERSON STRAIGHT

Throughout this book I've emphasized the importance of using your knowledge of human nature to build relationships with other people. I've also stressed the importance of learning enough about individuals to accurately read their intent. This leads to a principle that I'm guessing 99 percent of the population fails to practice: You can't tell what someone is trying to accomplish merely by observing their actions. And even when you think can read their intent, there's a great deal more to learn by listening to how they describe what they've done. Of course, you never think to ask about intent when people behave as you expect. The only time you inquire is when they act in ways that surprise you. Then you're likely to ask in a tone that implies the question: "Why in the world would you ever do that," giving the impression that you can't imagine yourself doing anything so dumb.

> You can't tell what someone is trying to accomplish merely by observing their actions.

Even when people say what you would say, or act as you would act, their reasons for doing so may be quite different from yours. People are distinctive in history and constitution. Driven by unique self-interests, they pursue different agendas, in the workplace and out. As a result, prior to critiquing a cohort's behavior I recommend your first finding out what your cohort was thinking when taking the actions you found ill advised. You might simply ask, "How come you decided to do it this way?" What you might perceive as "aggressive" or "hostile," the other person might describe as "self-protective" or an attempt to keep from feeling "judged." You'll get friendlier, richer, and more pointed answers when you echo the exact words your cohort used. Freud allegedly said, "Sometimes a cigar is just a good smoke," and well it might be. But people keep repeating this phrase because sometimes a cigar is symbolic of something else. Using the other person's terminology makes it easier to stay on the same page.

It's logical to assume your chances of communicating accurately are substantially greater with a straight-talk cohort than with someone with whom you usually exchange bullsh*t. Nevertheless, any communication, however simple, can readily become problematic. Even in a straight-talk relationship, it's wise to inquire when you get signals that the other person might not have received the message you intended to send. Keep in mind that any element of your cohort's past, including events about which you know nothing, can underlie his or her unexpected interpretation.

A line in the film *Magnolia* makes the point that what you're dealing with may entail substantially more than you can see on the surface. The line goes: "We might be through with the past, but it ain't [ever] through with us." This is something to keep in mind when your candor meets with a cohort's resistance. The past is never through with the other person, just as it's never through with you. Some of your cohort's reaction will relate to his or her life prior to meeting you. But your cohort's reaction may also be the result of his or her taking offense in the present. When you have an inkling that you may have offended, you can simply ask, "Should I be taking your reaction personally? Did I say something that offended you?" Do your best not to conclude slight, insult, or rejection without giving the other person the opportunity to clarify. Even when another person initially misspeaks, they can eventually tell you what they intended to communicate. What's more, you need to remember that your interpretation is no more objective than your cohort's response. You may have misheard what the other person said.

Some people think a straight-talk relationship is successful when all cohorts' viewpoints converge. I disagree. I see the test of a successful straight-talk relationship as its capacity to respectfully acknowledge differing viewpoints even after substantial dialogue and argument.

Maintaining a straight-talk relationship when different viewpoints fail to converge will depend on what else you and your cohort know about one another. When you are able to recognize the personal reasoning and history that accounts for the other person's position, there's a good chance you'll be able to "red circle" the difference and move on to more productive topics. But hashing out a substantive difference on an issue that has great importance to either of you seldom leads to a satisfying resolution, unless you know the life experiences that account for your discrepant views. Without such background knowledge, you're both inclined to talk half-empty, not half-full, about the other person's positions. The resulting tensions can shatter the relationship.

It's a mistake to think that a straight-talk relationship allows you to engage each and every topic with un-nuanced candor. Resist the temptation to respond directly to topics on which cohorts are unlikely to change their positions or behavior. Such landmine topics often include personal appearances, financial circumstance, politics, styles and tastes, choice of love mates, and health and physical limitations.

We all come with human imperfections, blind spots, and emotional vulnerabilities. You need to avoid topics you believe your cohort can't talk about open-mindedly. There'll be some issues you couldn't have taken up with Mother Teresa. And don't be fooled when your straight-talk cohort insists, with apparent sincerity, "I want to hear your unvarnished opinion about my comb-over." He doesn't. Keeping your wits about you, you can improvise an appropriate evasion: "Why is this matter of interest to you now?" Resist the temptation to use truth-telling as a weapon.

You should also try to avoid thinking that straight-talk cohorts should be better than they actually are. Remember that everyone comes with imperfections that they may have struggled a lifetime to overcome. You shouldn't minimize their struggle even if overcoming it would be a piece of cake for you. As a straight-talk cohort, you are expected to point out areas that need change, remembering that making the change is the sole responsibility of the other person. In fact, you'd do well to remember that your feedback will seldom be compelling enough to cause the other person to immediately change. You have to wait for people to change themselves.

Impatiently repeating a prescription that your cohort can't seem to implement becomes a turnoff in any relationship. Resist the temptation to nag. One way to avoid repeating yourself is to change your approach. Instead of reiterating what you think your cohort should do differently, ask questions that will help him or her figure out what's standing in the way of improvement. Get into their heads. Ask, "What are you inclined to do?" Then ask follow-up questions to find out why your cohort's answers make perfect sense to them. Practice *mind-set management* consulting. Make a visit to the "organization" where your cohort lives and works—the one that exists uniquely in his or her head.

Straight-talk relationships require updating and regular check-ins, particularly when you and your cohort are in touch only intermittently. Everyone's life is dynamic, all circumstances and realities are in constant flux. Just as you need your cohorts to update you, you need to push yourself to keep them informed. When someone asks, "What's up with you? How's it going?" make a genuine effort to fill them in. Resist the knee-jerk, "Nothing much. Same as usual." Be a role model by making the effort to give a substantive answer.

Two elements determine the quality of the feedback you give. The first is accuracy, how truthfully you state the message you send, remembering all you have to offer is the truth you know. Second is the cohort's belief he or she possesses the skills and discipline to implement the improvements implied by your comments. Unfortunately, too many people in straight-talk relationships operate as if *accuracy* alone were sufficient. They behave as if their straight-talk obligation is discharged once they state their message clearly and candidly. These people act as if modifying their comments in light of limitations on their cohorts' part somehow compromises the integrity of the feedback. But I think it's important to frame your comments to match what your cohort thinks he or she can practically accomplish. Save the rest of what you believe for another time when you can accomplish more.

In formulating your message you'll want to determine the line between telling enough of the truth and telling too little. You don't want to cross over into bullsh*t or worse, by overspinning for cohort acceptance or withholding too much to avoid information overload. Hopefully the three standards described in Chapter 7 will be useful in your making your determination. Your feedback should not make your cohort excessively vulnerable or damage their self-esteem. It shouldn't involve bending or truncating the truth-you-know to the point that some future communication is perceived as "substantially different" from the truth you're currently communicating. And you need to continue to look for opportunities to get the rest of the truth-you-know across to your cohort.

Chapter 5 recommends using I-speak when sharing your views with another. Now I'd like to recommend an extrapolation of I-speak, *situation-speak*, that is especially useful in touchy situations at work. When citing flawed performance, for example, it's less upsetting for the recipient if you keep your comments specific to the current instance, the situation that prompted your feedback at this time. Avoid making overly broad comments even when you are responding to behavior the person persistently does. Speaking broadly imputes your cohort's character and can communicate that you think there's something inside that person is immutably damaged or flawed. Don't say, "You always . . ." or "There you go again." People seldom think of themselves as *always* doing anything. No one wants to hear you tell them that they're "always missing your point," "taking things too personally," "stubborn," "talking too much," "always conflict adverse" or even that they're always "generous," "intelligent" or "self-sacrificing." And resist the urge to suggest that the troublesome behavior spills over into other areas of his or her life. You might ask something like, "Do you think some aspect of what we're talking about extends to the way you deal with your kids?" But let your cohort name the pattern and describe the impact it has. This way you improve the likelihood the relationship survives the difficult moment to provide insights that may benefit both of you in the future.

In work life, you'll find many situations where feedback is expected as part of performance reviews, team-building exercises, and other organizational activities. I advise rigorous caution and restraint in these situations if one of you is a chain-of-command direct report of the other. In terms of organizational performance, no mandated activity gets people and their organizations into more trouble than evaluation schemes that begin with a truth-as-it-exists assessment of the other person, no matter how close the cohorts. I even advise restraint when it comes to truth-as-it's-perceived-by-others schemes. The rule of thumb: never jump in without first getting your cohorts to articulate their self-view. Always angle yourself for an "I see it differently" response. Then you can be as blunt and direct as you find appropriate because you've left room for your cohort to contradict your assertions just as bluntly.

In summary, when it comes to looking out for cohorts and giving truth-on-demand feedback, all messages are subject to spin, shading, and other forms of adjustment. Integrity is not achieved by resisting compromise. It's achieved by resisting compromise beyond the point where you can honestly say to yourself, "I gave him as much of the truth as I thought he could stand." Whether the topic is what the other person has already done, has not done, or is presently doing, the only intelligent way to straight-talk is by first inquiring into the truth-the-other-person-knows. I know I'm repeating myself here. But too many people are inclined to begin giving advice with a truth-as-I-know-it account. Regardless of what convention and organizational practices dictate, you'll be much better off, and so will your straight-talk relationship, if the person being critiqued expresses the truth they know first and you start your reasoning from there.

11 STRAIGHT-TALK
Truth-Finding

Marko Rossi, a visiting professor from Italy, told me this story.

"I was up at my computer at 4:30 A.M. with an urgent assignment. Mannaggia! The computer doesn't turn on. I push it, I hit it, nothing. Time to call Dell Service. Fortunatamente I'm in luck. I get someone in Texas. Usually I get India. That taxes my English. I don't do well with accents. Now comes the work. The technician wants me under the desk disconnecting wires and taking off a side panel. How do I find a flashlight without waking Francesca? None of this is what I want to do. It's still dark, where's the stupido screwdriver?

"To the technician's credit it only takes 45 minutes to diagnosis the problem. My eight-month old PC needs a new motherboard. I can barely believe the solution. Within four hours a service man will bring and install a replacement. Given my disaster I'm feeling pretty good. But I start losing it when in response to my 'please reassure me' question the technician says, 'Yes, you might lose all your data.'

"The next thing I remember is the technician screaming, 'If you continue shouting at me, I'm going to hang up.' That came as a splash of cold water. I scream back, 'I'm not screaming, I'm Italian. And I'm not screaming at you. I'm screaming in pain because 5 o'clock in the morning I'm hearing I might lose my research, checkbook, and a few other small items like that. What would you do if someone told you all your data could go poof? Remember, in this disaster you're the only amico I got.'

"The buone notizie is I didn't lose a thing. But I keep thinking about the technician whose job it is to reassure trauma victims like me. I realize he has to cover his backside. Just so he could say he warned me, he gave me four hours with huge anxiety. Why couldn't this tipo get what was happening? Why is he taking any of this personally? It's clearly a situational problem. How come he doesn't get my realitá?"

I CALL THE PROCESS for connecting intent to behavior *truth-finding.* This is a technique for uncovering truth independently of what someone told you or what you saw them do. Whereas "bullsh*t," "truth-telling," and "lying" depend on what is going on in the communicator's mind, truth-finding involves the conclusions and truths created in the receiver's mind, with or without exposure to anyone else. Done poorly it's projection, not truth-finding, a fiction you, the recipient, made up.

But performed well, with discipline and rigor, truth-finding produces a high-grade reality that results from analysis of all previous communications and impressions, not just from a literal interpretation of what you observed taking place in the moment. It is the kind of analysis that allows you to discount a disappointed teenager's words when, in a moment of high frustration, he shouts, "I hate you, Dad." In the workplace, it is what allows you to decide that your boss is unlikely to keep a promise you just heard her make in all apparent sincerity. Truth-finding requires rolling up everything you know to create the big picture that surrounds what you are witnessing in the moment, coming to a conclusion, and conducting yourself accordingly.

Of course, everyone performs truth-finding to some degree, and some people are much better than others at figuring out the meaning behind what's taking place. Done properly, truth-finding is a disciplined process for linking other people's intentions with the words and behavior you observe them use. Sometimes you're able to make informed interpretations as you go along. Other times it takes a while to reflect on and then interpret what has taken place.

Truth-finding addresses the most fundamental question about human motives: "Why is this (fill in the *blank*) happening now?" The *blank* is anything that causes you to wonder what's behind a particular statement or action. It might be a puzzling statement, an emotional outburst, an off-the-cuff action—just about anything. In many instances, you'll determine that the behavior in question was totally unrelated to a person's relationship with you. In fact, too often people take personally what isn't directed at them. Truth-finding helps you distinguish between words and actions directed at you and those that are merely a product of the other person doing their "thing."

There are many truth-finding methodologies and no doubt you've got a favorite. Over the years I've developed two that have served me very well. I rely on them one at a time or simultaneously, as circumstances permit. You are probably familiar with aspects of each. The first—"Why this now?"—entails disciplined analysis using the powers of deductive reasoning. It's today's version of a format I developed in the 1970s. It evolved as I was trying to identify the corporate protocols and buried assumptions relating to counterproductive policies and prejudicial practices within companies. I was seeking a means for helping professionals and managers become more aware of the hidden directives that blocked them from doing their best, either for themselves or the company.[1] Had that methodology been applied more recently, it would have allowed someone eavesdropping on Enron traders to conclude that upper-echelon executives were complicit in the public bilking taking place. I have always found this method to be an extremely useful tool for uncovering non-apparent agendas.

The second method, *alignment tracking*, involves extrapolating from the big picture, life-story issues a person has faced in the past to determine the likely intent and meaning of behavior you observe in the present. This method involves relationship-building activities—something you should find the time to perform with everyone who plays a prominent role in your life, at work or outside. You may even want to engage in such activities with people who are peripheral at the moment, but who you think you might be working with at some future time.

Alignment tracking involves both inductive reasoning and "active questioning." Unfortunately, active questioning is not a skill taught in most MBA curriculums. However, it is a skill that's relatively easy to master once you understand the model. It's also a useful complement to "active listening," which most MBA curriculums tout to be a valued mainstream skill.

WHY THIS NOW?

When you find yourself suspicious, or have the feeling you're being asked to endorse a hidden agenda, you should ask yourself a strategic question: "Why is 'this' happening now?" Reasoning through this question has the potential to reveal most of what you want to know. Of note is that only three key words are involved.

"Why" is the first key word. It leads your inquiry in the direction it needs to go. "Why?" contrasts with "What?"—a question that's more commonly asked. Most people ask: "What's happening? What's going on here?" Such questions are common, but asking "what" can be misleading. "*What?*" leads a person to *react*, which puts the cart of action before the horse of intent. By focusing on intent, "*Why?*" is likely to produce far more useful information. Determining intent is the appropriate starting point for everything that comes after. Only after you know what another person intends, and the reasoning that led them to say and do what they did, should you start thinking about your response.

This process brings to mind an old saying: "If you want to know what a moose is doing, you first need to know how a moose thinks." And communications from humans are considerably more complicated than those from a moose. Even if you're talking with your separated-at-birth Siamese twin, the only thing you know for sure is that he thinks and reasons differently from you. Only after you understand the intent behind what you've witnessed, can you intelligently plan your response.

"This" is the second key word in this analytical process. It is a ___blank___ to be filled in. "This" might be an awkward comment, a surprising emotion, an unexpected acquiescence, a drop-by visit, or almost anything else. It can be anything that doesn't seem to fit into the ordinary pattern of your dealings with another person. Simply spelling out what you mean by "this" will produce valuable clues. If a verbal communication seems off, you might ask yourself: "Why does she think it important to send me 'this' message?" If actions are baffling, say perhaps an unexpected deviation from an agreed-on larger plan of activity, then the appropriate question might be: "Why does he find it necessary to take 'this' action?" And the "this" may even be a failure to act, leading to such questions as "Why isn't this person participating?" "Why is he so stuck?" "Why isn't he backing me on this issue?" "Why didn't the signed agreement arrive in the mail as was promised?"

You often find that the "this" is actually typical of someone's reactions to a category of situations, and that discovery can be a revelation. Are you dealing with someone who is often uptight, controlling, or unnecessarily belligerent? Or has something specific taken place that accounts for that person's aggressive reaction? You need to discriminate between what's directed at you and what the other person frequently does in situations like the current one.

"Now" is the third key word. It is a reminder that the surprising behavior was the end result of your cohort's mental processes. It cues you to think about the sequence of events that, in the other person's mind, produced the need to initiate what you just heard or observed. For example, you might ask, what was going on in the other person's head that led them to send a communication bearing on an agenda that they didn't want you to know they were pursuing? Did something happen to make the other person feel the need to influence you or did the other person simply misspeak? You don't want to cause yourself or those who misspeak unnecessary problems by reacting personally to an inept tangle of words that's of no real consequence to you. Such an analysis would have helped the Dell technician dealing with my Italian friend. Instead of reacting to Marko's expressions of fear, the technician might have reasoned himself into a more accurate reading of Marko's alarmed outburst. Marko's upset had nothing to do with the technician personally. The technician just happened to be a bystander in the presence of an understandably fearful person with an emotional temperament.

There's also a facet of "Why this now?" analysis that focuses on you. Unfortunately, it's not the whole, multifaceted "you" of your reality. It's a truncated, stripped-down, facsimile of "you" determined by the role you play in the communicator's mind at the moment you interacted. No doubt there are situations where the communicator thinks about you quite differently. But in order to determine intent, you need to limit yourself to the version of you implied in the actions that caught your eye. You need to figure out the role you have been assigned in the drama the other person is living. Often, that "you" has less to do with the real you and more to do with someone in that person's past. For example, you might experience a series of put-downs and feel an unexpected territorial protectiveness from a peer who normally seems to view you as a collaborative, competent teammate. From this you might deduce that in her mind she is competing with you to become leader on a new project. Once you realize that and begin thinking about it, you may discover that you don't even want that leadership role. This might lead you to decide that there's little need to fight her for the role—especially in light of the fact that she already knows you are no pushover. You might ultimately decide you are best served by making her aware that you support her leadership bid.

> You need to figure out the role you have been assigned in the drama the other person is living.

Two other kinds of data may be uncovered in the course of a "Why this now?" question. First, you may be able to identify underlying self-assumptions implied by the actions that caught your interest. Simply ask yourself, "What can I learn about how this individual sees him- or herself from the way that he or she is now behaving?" Second, you may be able to identify the implicit organizational and system assumptions underscoring this behavior. You'll find inductive reasoning useful in this process. You might ask yourself: "What can I learn about how this person sees the organization from his or her need to act this way or take this approach?" You might find what you learn an informed addition to your own view of the company.

ALIGNMENT MODEL AND ACTIVE QUESTIONING
Most people will give you an open-book view of their lives if you know the right questions to ask and if you make your

inquiries *before* your relationship becomes problematic. Even people communicating covert bullsh*t will often divulge revealing personal history. Most people are willing, even eager, to tell you what is and has been important in their lives. And because people bring their personal histories to work, you have a good chance of extrapolating what you have learned about the person to workplace situations that involve you.

Years ago Jack McDonough and I formulated a model for characterizing and learning about the unique orientations people impose on their work. Our model is based on understanding how personal background, self-concept, values, and life goals affect everyday actions. The model postulates a continual interaction between personal expressiveness and what an individual feels obligated to accomplish for the company, by virtue of receiving a paycheck, his or her work ethic, and his or her need to be seen as competent, constructive, and valuable. The model shows that people continually gerrymander their assignments to fit both what they find personally interesting and meaningful and what they can competently do. It also shows them morphing what they find personally meaningful to fit with job satisfactions they perceive to be attainable. The morphing is dynamic. People modify their work functions until they reach a point where they think any further change will cause them to lose credibility or to be ineffective. People also modify the list of satisfactions they seek. Eventually, they adapt and come to value those that are actually available to them until typically they reach a point where they are no longer dealing with a version of themselves that seems self-meaningful. It's understandable why people make such adjustments. After all, any job description designed by someone else reflects what that person wants, not necessarily the talents and desires of the person filling the position.

We called the model "Alignment" to emphasize the unique and distinctive orientations people come up with in attempting to *align* lifelong pursuits with what they see as required by their job. See Figure 1 below. Appendix A presents a set of relatively easy-to-answer questions that you can ask to determine an individual's alignment and to describe the orientation an individual has adopted. The model allows you to follow the thinking that leads to specific agendas pursued. The model facilitates intelligent speculation about what specific actions reflect what intentions and why people proceed as they do, even if past experience should have taught them the futility of some approaches.

The alignment questions can reveal a person's philosophy of life, beliefs about their personal resources, self-perceived deficiencies, and ambitions. Each question elicits information about personal history, values, attitudes, and agendas. When instructing MBA students to use these questions, I urge them to probe for the personal meanings behind the answers received. For instance, people are asked to name their role models and anti-models. In a follow-up question, the respondent is asked to name the characteristics to be emulated or avoided and then to explain why those characteristics hold so much personal importance for them. Another question is: "What was the last

Personal Productivity and Meaning	Organizational Productivity and Meaning
• Utilize personal skills	Produce what the
• Avoid non-skills	individual believes the
• Pursue interests	organization should
• Embody values	be receiving from
• Express personality and indulge quirks	someone occupying his or her role and
• Meet personal commitments	position

FIGURE 1   Alignment model for covert truth-telling.

personally important life lesson learned?" The follow-up qu tion asks why it took so long to learn a lesson that others, wi different backgrounds and life circumstances, learned earlie in their lives and with greater ease. Of course, the follow-up questions require that you know what information you are after. The alignment model helps you identify aspects of other people that are key to demystifying their behavior.

As I tell my students, it is vitally important to understand the basis for someone else's thinking, and the best way to do that is by sensitively probing for information. I call the process *active questioning.* It is quite different from the passive or aggressive questioning that people often do when they're unsure of what they're looking for or don't respect the sensitivities of their informants. In my mind, active questioning is the necessary complement of open-minded listening. Complete instructions for using the questions in Appendix A are contained in Chapters 6 and 7 of *Mind-Set Management.*

The alignment model provides a realistic way of thinking about the uniqueness of personal styles. In my view, this personalized model is far more useful than such popular but essentially empty approaches as "uniform best practices." Instead of trying to impose "uniform best practices" on everyone, we might ask the question: "What does this person intend to accomplish and why does he or she go about it this way?" Our model challenges the notion that one-size-fits-all metrics are meaningful. Instead, it provides a new framework for improving performance and effectiveness—by discovering the variables that underlie the individual's behavior and using that knowledge in appreciating performance and in thinking about enhancements that the performer will find appropriate.

In virtually every workplace, people are critiqued against standardized metrics that are alleged to be based on how a rational mind sees what is objectively required to perform the task effectively. But externally imposed metrics fail to take human needs and individuality into account. Their existence is at variance with the fact that numerous and unique factors drive the actions a person takes. They cause evaluators to come to conclusions that have little or no bearing on how a human being actually goes about his or her job. The use of preconceived metrics makes workplace evaluation, at best, a farce and, worse, demoralizing pretense. It is a rare evaluator who thinks to ask each individual to explain the uniqueness in the way they go about being their best in meeting the productive needs of the company. In fact, most evaluators don't even know what questions to ask in staging for a subordinate's most effective performance. Recall they include "How are you going about it?" "What obstacles do you face?" and "What do you need from me?"

> The use of preconceived metrics makes workplace evaluation, at best, a farce and, worse, demoralizing pretense.

If you could know everything about a person's life, you would find that people operate according to a rationality all their own. But most bosses never look below or beyond the surface in learning the personal history and unique talents and traits that account for how someone performs their job. If bosses, and colleagues, took the trouble to inquire about personal facts and the basis for values held, they would get a truer sense of why specific others behave as they do. Without knowing what others truly value and intend, we are all prone to fill in the gaps with projections and projections produce misleading conclusions. The result is a workplace in which most people are frustrated too much of the time, and so much less is accomplished than could be.

CONCLUSION

Mysteries of the moment dissolve as you learn more about another person and better appreciate the roles they assign you in the agendas they pursue at work. Don't be put off if you can't immediately "read" what they are saying or doing. Your confusion doesn't necessarily mean that the other person's interests are incompatible with yours or even that they are trying to slip one past you. This chapter has provided techniques you can use to probe beneath the surface to learn more about the intentions and values of others *before* you react. Use inductive reasoning asking the question: "Why this now?" Master alignment tracking and active questioning as techniques for truth-finding. Both processes require maintaining an open mind, which is probably your most valuable truth-finding tool. The reward for this effort will be insight into the other person's truth that will allow you to advance your agendas more effectively.

CONCLUSION

12

STRAIGHT-TALK

It Pays to Advertise

Explaining why Syrians would speak candidly to a Jewish-American reporter at the height of Israeli attacks on Hezbollah strongholds in Lebanon, Tom Friedman said, "just showing up is a sign of respect." He added: "if I've found one thing as a reporter, and I've worked in the Arab world for 25 years, I've found listening is a sign of respect. If you just go over and listen to people and what they have to say, it's amazing what they'll allow you to say back."[1]

WHATEVER YOUR COMPANY ROLE, whenever you encounter others, you probably want them to see you as a person with whom they can openly talk straight. Everyone has their own ways of encouraging that belief. Some people smile and nod a lot, some are quick to compliment, some perform favors, some ask provocative questions, some practice "tell me more" listening, some point out similarities in background or interests—each person has favorite methods. If there's any mystery in the process, it is what goes on in the mind of a recipient that makes a particular communicator's distinctive style so appealing.

In addition to these individual styles, there is one approach that has almost universal appeal. That is when someone lowers their guard to act natural, allowing their human qualities and vulnerabilities to show through. People almost always trust that. When someone seems to be comfortable in their own skin, eschews pretense, and seems willing to dispense with the standard organizational bullsh*t, others tend to view them as sincere. Others are likely to accept the communicator's imperfections and, in turn, speak more candidly themselves.

There's a new buzzword going around that bears on this topic: *mokita*. Googling it I learned it's alleged to be a New Guinean word that means "the truth everyone knows but no one speaks." In the Western world, examples of *mokita* include personal biases, human imperfection, self-interest as the dominant driver of human behavior, and the routine use of garden variety *bullsh*t* in smoothing over and avoiding interpersonal friction. Most of the time you can avoid talking about these hidden truths but eventually that leads to miscommunication, suspicion, and a host of other negative consequences. Alternatively, you aren't likely to draw a crowd by hanging an "I'm a straight-talker" sign on your door. Too much one-sided candor causes people to self-protectively close down. To a greater or lesser degree, all people need tangible evidence before they leap to the belief that you are someone with whom they can safely talk straight.

In earlier chapters, you found many guidelines for forming straight-talk relationships. What can't be predicted in advance is what unique scheme will work best for you. That requires your own invention. You need to find an approach that harmonizes with your distinctive nature, inimitable personality, and style. This is imperative since others will be scrutinizing your words and behavior for authenticity and congruence with the truth they believe. They'll be especially alert when they see you participating in one of the standard corporate charades. Perhaps the test of your credibility will come when they see you giving a performance review using conventional metrics, instead of measures aligned with an employee's talents, needs, and values. Perhaps it will come when they resist an agenda you propose that's inconsistent with what they're after. They probably won't admit that's their reason for resisting—since they too participate in the charade that everything we do here at Company X is for the greater good of the corporation. People expect some measure of bullsh*t at work; that's the corporate way. But if they decide you are insensitive to what matters to them, that you are somehow disconnected from your human nature, or that you are unaware that what you are doing is actually pretense, you will fail their test, that's guaranteed.

Throughout the text, I've emphasized the importance of distinguishing straight-talk from other ostensibly honest formats. I've argued that no truth-telling takes place independently of relationship, context, or agenda pursued. I've asserted that the truth of a message is not absolute but a function of its timing, the credibility of the communicator, and the recipient's interpretation of it. And I've put forth guidelines for maximizing the likelihood that your own communications will succeed and for increasing your ability to "read" someone else's words and actions by analyzing for intent.

Remaining to be discussed are three aesthetic qualities that have the potential to substantially enhance your ability to engage others in straight-talk relationships. The first is *sincere interest in and curiosity about the personal lives* of the people you meet. The second is *greeting people with an open heart*. And the third is exhibiting a *non-collusive style of loyalty*. These qualities are not easily faked. Nor are they qualities everyone will immediately recognize when you exhibit them.

Of the three, *loyalty* is the only quality people expect at work, notwithstanding the fact that they rarely get the non-collusive kind they actually need. On the other hand, neither *sincere interest* nor *open-heartedness* is a quality people usually extend to others, or even expect to receive, in the workplace. When such qualities are expressed, they are often seen as charades undertaken for political convenience. For example, sincere interest and open-heartedness are feigned in most first meetings with new work associates, occasions when people try especially hard to make a good impression.

Both "sincere interest" and "open-heartedness" are qualities much more likely to be expressed in non-work settings. At work people expect level-headed rational engagement, not warm intimate encounters. And people expect work-focused conversations without "intrusive" inquiries into their personal lives. Nonetheless, when others see you displaying these qualities, and sense that you are doing so sincerely, you instantly make a straight-talk relationship more likely.

LOYALTY

When I ask people what they expect in the way of loyalty, I often hear about a brand that borders on workplace collusion. I hear about expectations of unquestioning allegiance and pacts cemented by the implied promise that "I'll make sure you get to keep your job." These smack of what psychologists call *unconditional positive regard*[2]—a quality most adults complain about not receiving enough of when they were children. Simply stated, unconditional regard translates into, "I love and value you even when I disapprove of what you're doing." It contrasts with *conditional regard*, which translates into, "I love and value you when what you are doing pleases me but not when you behave in ways I don't like." If most adults couldn't get unconditional regard from parents who loved them, why would they think they could get it at work from people pursuing competitive agendas who love them far less than their parents did? In a self-interested world, even fantasizing about unconditional positive regard entails first fooling yourself. Next, it means engaging in you-rub-my-back-I'll-rub-yours political collusion. To expect loyalty and support, no matter what is accomplished or how your agendas align with those of others, is simply not a realistic expectation in a free-market-economy workplace.

The loyalty people need is based more on truthfulness and less on the total commitment loyalty most individuals seek. People need loyalty in the form of support, cooperation, and encouragement, contributions that can actually help them to perform more effectively. They need loyalty in the form of delivering what you promise, noticing and valuing their positive qualities, acknowledging their contributions, and sharing your opinions forthrightly, as openly and honestly as circumstances allow. This brand of loyalty is sometimes demonstrated merely by telling someone, "I'm not in a position to be up front stating my true beliefs at this time." This brand of loyalty is manifest when you acknowledge someone's positive qualities and good intentions while recommending how they might perform more effectively or telling them straight out that you will not support them if they take the actions they are contemplating.

I-speak is invaluable for successfully expressing this kind of loyalty. I-speak almost always engenders a positive response. Better people should hear: "I can't comfortably tell you that" or "I can't accommodate your wishes now" than to be misled by your silence thinking that you are willing to support what they are planning to say or do when you are not. Very importantly, the brand of loyalty I'm advocating also includes making sure that involved others have a voice in affairs that concern them and giving open-minded consideration to their viewpoints even when their agendas run counter to what you propose. This is very different from seeming to agree or pretending to go along when you have no intention of doing so. That, of course, is bullsh*t.

The loyalty I've just described is less rigorous than what is required in a true straight-talk relationship. But as with straight-talk, there's serious consideration of the truth-you-know prior to giving a response, and efforts are made to make sure others have an adequate opportunity to express their views. It differs from straight-talk in that there's no obligation to explicitly state all the truths you believe or to diligently track the other person's self-interested agendas with a commitment to help. In the workplace, there are many times when you don't want people whom you can't hold accountable to know your personal views. At those moments, your loyalty might require nothing more than not stating a non-truth nor misleading with covert bullsh*t.

SINCERE INTEREST IN AND CURIOSITY ABOUT SOMEONE'S LIFE

Journalist Tom Friedman is a prime example of someone who is able to elicit candor from people very different from himself through sincere interest in and curiosity about their lives. He understands that if you're interested in straight-talk, the absolute best thing you can do is listen. But it's not passive listening. That's never been Tom Friedman's style. His style involves active listening, combined with *active questioning*, all with both an open mind and an open heart. Active questioning is needed to uncover the personal history that accounts for why another person reacts the way he or she does. It's critical for understanding intent. Only when you probe beneath the surface to understand intent, do the actions other people take truly begin to make sense.

> If you're interested in straight-talk, the absolute best thing you can do is listen.

I've found that people—even those who behave as if they couldn't care less if they were well liked—become less guarded when someone greets them warmly and shows a genuine interest in learning about their life. I'm not talking here about the old-fashioned practice of a boss asking, "How's the Mrs.? How did her mother's visit go?" I'm talking about a sincere interest in the other person's human qualities and general well-being, an interest on your part that leads to thoughtful inquiry, acts of friendship, confidence-keeping, and other proofs of authentic regard. I'm talking about exchanges that make room for personal feelings and leave you feeling enriched by working alongside people you truly care about. I'm talking about inviting people over to your home or to your daughter's soccer game for a get-to-know-you-better conversation and the bonding that results.

Your willingness to spend time developing these bonds depends on your recognizing two aspects of human nature. The first is that each person's life is full of important life lessons that you may not have already learned. Inquiring about an individual's life and its challenges has the potential to teach you lessons that turn out to be invaluable.

The second aspect of human nature to keep in mind is that everyone, even your heroes, comes fully equipped with shortcomings that are usually more obvious to you than to them. Moreover, when you see a short suit in someone else that bothers you more than it seems to bother others, chances are it's either because it gets in the way of your own self-interested pursuits or it's a short suit that you yourself also possesses.

"Why this now?" reasoning gives you a way to transform your recognition of someone's shortcoming into a useful lesson for yourself. You merely ask yourself, "Why is this person's human-foible deficiency irritating me so much right now?" At the end you may still find the attribute annoying, but the process of reflection may diminish some of the negativity you feel toward that person. What's more, you can count on others watching when such frustrations arise at work. They'll be wondering what they will face if they ever rub you the wrong way. They will be especially interested in whether you can keep the other person's positive attributes in mind when dealing with a limitation that bothers you.

When others see you trying to expand your knowledge of the human condition—trying to better equip yourself to deal with future challenges—they're more likely to see your interest in them as sincere. They will also respond positively when they realize that your interest in any of their deficiencies connects to an idiosyncratic need or sensitivity of your own. People like it when they see you scrutinizing their lives for lessons to use in enhancing your own. They find this existentially affirming.

Inquiring into the private lives of others requires some delicacy, but using even minimal finesse you'll seldom rub them the wrong way. There's no topic most people would rather talk about than themselves. They just need to feel emotionally and politically safe. You know this to be true because you feel the same way. If the conventions of the workplace only allowed it, we could launch many more straight-talk relationships simply by saying, "Tell me about your life."

There are any number of situation-appropriate questions you might ask to get people to share stories about their lives. Any of the alignment questions listed in Appendix A can get you started. The more people confide, the more they'll be able to determine whether or not you are a person they can trust. Beware of asking these probing questions and then interrupting the other person's answers. Don't use their answers as an excuse to talk about yourself or engage in other conversation stoppers. You'd be better off if you never tried to gain their trust. When advertising for straight-talk, every conversation becomes an audition.

OPEN-HEARTEDNESS

Open-heartedness requires spiritual generosity. I'm talking about tolerating other's imperfections and being slow to draw negative conclusions when someone carelessly hurts your feelings or impedes your progress. These things usually happen when people act in their own interest without you or your sensitivities on their mental map. You sometimes do the same thing. Even the best intentioned people sometimes act with ADD-like self-focus. In fact, a larger percentage of people than you may realize cope with ADD, anxiety, mood swings, dyslexia, memory difficulties, or other problems that affect their interactions with others. And that doesn't even take into account temperamental and psychological differences.

Opening your heart entails giving everyone a second, third, and even fourth chance. To do so you'll find it useful to engage in active questioning. You need to find ways of learning more about a person who inadvertently steps on your toes. The usual techniques should suffice. First ask the other person their views of what happened. Use I-speak to own your perceptions. Don't be accusatory. Analyze their intent and then analyze it again seeing if you can envision a positive motive. Finally, always elicit and listen to different viewpoints. Take the other person aside. Ask something like, "I don't know why this happened, but when you said/did ___fill in the blank___ my feelings were hurt." Or you might say, "I don't know if you were aware of what I was trying to accomplish, but when you said ___fill in the blank___ I felt blocked and feared my words and efforts were being discounted." Say what you have to say; then stop talking. To some extent your words have already put the other person on the defensive so it's counterproductive to say more. If, in response, the other person communicates bullsh*t or tries to fool you with a lie, it may be in your best interest to be generous and let them off the hook. Treat self-protective responses as throwaway lines—remember, your statement may have sounded accusatory and your willingness to engage them directly may have taken them by surprise. Then watch their subsequent actions. You'll be surprised how often the other person eventually appreciates your raising a sticky issue or implicitly extends an olive branch by acting differently next time.

Inquiring about people's lives almost always leads you to realizations you had no advance way of anticipating. For example, I often reflect on an experience I had in Japan that taught me an unexpected lesson about human nature. It began as a chance encounter I had in the Tokyo subway on my first assignment in Japan. I had just read Ruth Benedict's classic book on Japanese culture, *The Chrysanthemum and the Sword*.[3] At the time I thought the lesson distinctively Japanese. Subsequently I realized it was a lesson that applies to Westerners as well.

It was rush hour, and I was following written instructions to a Procter & Gamble facility. I had gotten myself turned around and was having trouble figuring out which train line to take and in what direction. I tried asking for assistance but the platform was so crowded that I couldn't even get enough space between myself and anyone else to make eye contact. Not speaking the language, I didn't know how to get anyone's attention. Then someone bumped me, and I dropped my folder. Bending down to retrieve it, I almost smashed head to head with a man who was picking it up for me. Thanking him, I seized the opportunity to ask for directions. Unfortunately, I'm afraid I also ruined his morning. Instead of just giving me directions, he felt obligated to take me to my destination.

Guiding me through a series of tunnels, he led me to the correct line. Then, despite my repeatedly telling him, "*Arigato*, I'm okay," he boarded the train and rode with me to my stop. We got off the train, he smiled, we exchanged bows, and then he walked to a different line. That's the last I saw of him.

Mulling over the experience and thinking about the Benedict book, I realized why it had been so difficult to get a stranger's attention when I was lost in the subway station. Apparently, in Japan, giving assistance comes with an obligation to be responsible for the well-being of the person you assist. The Japanese word is *giri*. Giving directions was not enough. My Good Samaritan couldn't take the chance I might not successfully follow them—he was now responsible for my getting where I needed to go.

This experience helped me understand the camaraderie Westerners feel toward someone they have befriended and helped. You might think a person you helped now owes you one—the "principle of reciprocity." However, as I was reminded in the Tokyo Underground, helping someone frequently implants feelings of obligation and loyalty in the helper. The takeaway for our purposes, as odd as it may sound, is that opening your heart includes letting others help you. I'm not talking about abject "dependency." I'm talking about expressing vulnerability, graciously accepting assistance from others, and always explicitly crediting them for their contributions. I've always thought there were parallels here with leadership. Leading requires followers, and the leader should be aware of and grateful for that complementary relationship. It's also the underlying premise of "mentorship." The more someone helps you, the stronger their allegiance to you grows.

People prosper when engaged in collegial, give-and-take relationships, and that's part of the appeal and pleasure of straight-talk. Even when someone believes they're in the presence of an expert or hierarchical big shot, they want their own human qualities seen and prized. People want a personal connection to what's going on. They are drawn to those who seem to value them for their naturalness and humanity so much that they want that connection even when listening to a speech in a large auditorium. I recall attending a presentation given by a former student who had acquired a reputation as an outstanding motivational speaker. Her captivating quality was apparent the moment she began to speak. She began by relating some of the mistakes she had made on the topic she was presenting. She seemed utterly authentic. Five minutes in, everyone was on her side, eager to apply what she recommended, almost without noticing things she said that a reasonable person might disagree with or doubt. I was surprised at how powerfully recounting her struggles connected her to the audience. It was her authenticity, as much as her expertise, that endowed her words with authority.

I have a different way of connecting to an audience. I like to be informal and mock the pretensions of everyday life. I'm a bit like an old-time comedian who stumbles to get a laugh when coming out on stage. I tell funny anecdotes about myself and share ironies of my life to illustrate principles I want to teach. This approach almost always provides me a feeling of connection with the audience; it helps me deal with childhood feelings of not having adults around whom I could count on to look out for me. That childhood, and subsequent experiences, gave me a lifelong sensitivity to inequities in relationships. In every situation I work like crazy to establish parity among the participants. I don't want anyone in a meeting or audience to feel unnecessarily marginal or one-down.

Each person has a unique story to tell and a distinctive style to express. I can't help wondering how *you* will go about getting more straight-talk at work. How are you going to eliminate needless bullsh*t? How will you let others know when you're eager for straight-talk? I hope this book will help you make the most of your daily opportunities. I only wish I could be there to see you enjoy the benefits of straight-talk relationships at work.

APPENDIX A
Alignment Questions[1]

1. BUM RAP

Think of a "bum rap" or stereotype that someone has used in characterizing you and your limitations. State what goes unrecognized when you are portrayed this way, or what is unfair, and explain why the criticisms implied in this portrayal are too simplistic or categorical. State whether you have taken any action to counteract this exaggerated representation of you. If you have, what did you do? If not, why haven't you challenged this characterization?

2. INTENTION

What are you now trying to prove or demonstrate to others or to yourself? Explain why proving this is important. Then, if possible, describe an incident that illustrates how what you are trying to prove is reflected in your behavior.

3. WORK SUCCESS

Describe a work assignment that you take particular pride in having performed as well as you did (perhaps one from a former job or position). What was the personal significance to this accomplishment? What strengths or capacities were demonstrated? How were you challenged? Were any self-doubts involved? What does this accomplishment illustrate about your upbringing and what you had to overcome as an adult?

4. SELF-DISAPPOINTMENT

Now it's time to look at the other side of the coin. Describe a work assignment (current or from a former job or position) in which you failed to live up to expectations (yours or someone else's). How did you fail to perform? What was the disappointment? How do you explain why your performance failed to accomplish what you wanted to demonstrate or achieve?

5. ORGANIZATIONAL NEEDS

Currently, what does your organization *actually* need most from you and your job? To what extent are you able to provide it? Does providing this match with your personal needs for meaning? How so?

6. IMAGE

At work, how do you want to be seen? What image do you want to project? Are you aware of discrepancies between what you want to project and how others actually see you? What are those discrepancies? What are the chances that projecting your preferred image will be seen and valued by the people with whom you work, and that you'll be rewarded in your organization for possessing it? What needs to be accomplished for you to achieve that image?

7. WORK REWARDS

At work, what do you get that you want, and how do you ensure that you receive it? What do you get that you don't want, and what needs to happen for you to be more successful avoiding it? What do you *not* get that you *do* want and what needs to happen for you to get it?

8. ROLE MODELS

List the people you use as role models. For each one, state what qualities or skills you seek to emulate. Next name the people who have been anti-models for you, and their qualities or ways of operating that have provided you with reasons to operate differently.

9. WORLDVIEW

What do you believe is special and distinctive about how you see the world and interact with others? Give an example of how you view events distinctively. How does holding this worldview help you capitalize on your strengths and distinctive resources?

10. BACKGROUND AND PERSONAL CONSIDERATIONS

Tell something about your early upbringing and growing up that continues to play a strong role in determining how you function at work and what you seek.

11. WHERE ARE YOU HEADED?

What's ahead for you? Where are you heading personally, professionally, and family-wise? What does your vision of "tomorrow" entail? Be specific in describing your objectives. Do you need to make a change to attain them? If so, what changes will you need to make? In short, what do you need to start doing and to stop doing in order to realize long-term objectives and life goals?

12. AFTER YOU'RE GONE

How do you want to be remembered by the people with whom you work most closely? How do you want to be remembered by your immediate family and intimate friends? What unifying inscription would you like to have on your tombstone?

13. WHAT'S LEFT OUT?

Name a personal quality or strength that's frequently omitted or compromised in your present assignment. Provide an example of where this omission occurs.

14. LESSONS LEARNED

What was the last significant lesson you learned that changed the way you operate at work or how you relate with others? Why did it take as long as it did for you to learn? What's the next life or work lesson that you need to learn and internalize well enough to actually change and transform your actions? Explain why this has been difficult lesson for you to get straight.

15. ORIENTING OTHERS

What advice would you give to someone you were hiring to be your assistant about how to appreciate you, how to interact with you, and how to get your attention when your way of operating poses a problem for them?

ACKNOWLEDGMENTS

If you got this far, odds are that you're either a relative or someone who liked this book. Personally, I liked writing it a lot. The content flowed naturally from lessons I learned both on the job and from the rest of life. In the process, I was touched by the generous help I received from so many friends, and I want to acknowledge their contributions.

First is my wife Rosella. Her mere presence brings me joy. She contributed what she has been giving me from almost the first day we met: intellect, a keen aesthetic sense, and the unconditional love I yearned for as a child. I'm not easy to live with when I'm writing and Rosella seemed never to hold my frequent distraction against me. Because of her, I count myself one of the luckiest guys in the world.

Next come my close friend and colleague Warren Bennis and my editor extraordinaire Pat Biederman. Warren is one of my two every Sunday morning dates. We've been holding "psyche-sessions" regularly for fourteen years. These are fluid straight-talking discussions reflecting on our lives in general as well as projects of the moment. This last year's included the organization and content of this book. Outside of our meetings Warren spent considerable time reading and commenting on a next to last draft manuscript. Those who know Warren readily acknowledge he's a man of style, insight, and grace. In fact when he throws a festschrift it's 300 of society's elite contributors describing how their work benefited from what they learned from this Master. It's now been forty years since we first met. From our initial meeting, I could describe the same.

Pat Biederman is a gifted writer, journalist, and author. If I was the manuscript "decider," she was the pruner and polisher. I wish I had met her forty years ago. I prize the copy her blue pencil touched. Reading her markings was more than a good edit, it was instruction I try put to daily use—even when writing e-mails. At the time I didn't tell her how complimented I felt when a paragraph I wrote slipped by without a mark.

Elyse Montiel helped enormously on the initial drafting. She diligently read, commented, and encouraged me as the manuscript began to take shape. She often helped me say clearly what I was fumbling to put into words. At the same time I received generous and insightful counsel from Biren Sheh. A student who distinguished himself in two of my classes, he helped in the outlining of topics I wanted to include in the book. He also read and made extremely useful comments on early drafts.

It hasn't been fourteen years since I began meeting Sundays holding "personal life strategy sessions" with Mark Shahriary, but it will be eventually. We even meet after working all week on a project together. If Mark weren't a Ph.D. applied physicist, he'd be an oracle in a cave, philosopher and societal problem-solver. I relish the economy of our exchanges. Without losing nuance, Mark gets right to the point in terms I immediately understand. While I'd be hard-pressed to say precisely all that he contributed, I sense his presence on every page. He is my role model for professional partnering and supporting the others on your team.

There were so many other contributors that I barely know where to start or end. Looking back, it seems as if I spent two years convening impromptu focus groups for the book. When in the mood for feedback I reach out to everyone around. Noteworthy help was received from former Ph.D. students, who are now are now professors, deans, and consultants, including Jean-Francois Coget, Scott Schroeder, John Ullmen, Oscar Ortsman, and Susan Nero. Many of my straight-talk cohorts at UCLA and on consulting projects also took the time to read, edit, and comment. These include Brian Bennett, Eric Bergman, Phil Kleweno, Maia Young, Ralph Brooks, and Kalon Gutierrez.

Over the years my four children have learned to stand back and get out of the way when I'm writing a book. Perhaps they worry that the manuscript might contain covert messages intended for them. Like any bullsh*t artist, that's seldom what's on my mind. Looking back, I can see some basis for their concerns. Nevertheless, my son Gar, the academic, ventured out to lend an initial hand. I was moved by his courage and appreciated the clarity of his feedback. I've always found Gar a talented writer.

I've been talking straight with Ilene Kahn Powers for over fifty years. This is despite the fact that she's 49 and looks 37. (Did I say that straight Ilene?) She's a gifted writer, director, and award-winning producer. On a script or a manuscript, she's more than an editor. She is a commentator and, as she has for several of my books, provided an extremely valuable "read."

Academic colleague Walt Nord made a very special contribution. You name the topic or describe the phenomena, and he can point you to the scholarly literature that comments on it best. His range and depth of knowledge is extraordinary. And unlike so many with theoretical footings, he eschews airy jargon. This is the second manuscript he has vetted for me prior to its publication. His sincerity and integrity are always recognizably present. I can't think of a place where I failed to use his critique.

Finally I want to acknowledge Margo Beth Crouppen—the SUP editor who recruited my manuscript with her winning intellect and tasteful display of style and energy. This is the beginning of our journey together. I easily could go into detail but the bottom line is that I find her talents wonderfully complement mine and I really trust her. And Margo, if you're listening, "What have you done for me today?"

NOTES

PROLOGUE

1. S. A. Culbert and J. B. Ullmen, *Don't Kill the Bosses!* (San Francisco: Berrett-Koehler, 2001).

2. S. A. Culbert, *Mind-Set Management* (New York: Oxford University Press, 1996).

CHAPTER 1

1. First stated in Chapter 1 of *Radical Management: Power, Politics and the Pursuit of Trust*, S. A. Culbert and J. J. McDonough, New York: Free Press, 1985.

2. H. G. Frankfurt, *On Bullshit* (Princeton, NJ: Princeton University Press, 2005).

L. Penny, *Your Call Is Important To Us: The Truth About Bullshit* (New York: Crown, 2005).

B. Bodaken and R. Fitz, *The Management Moment of Truth* (New York: Free Press, 2006).

D. J. Lieberman, *Never Be Lied To Again* (New York: St. Martin's, 1998).

B. M. Patten, *Truth, Knowledge or Just Plain Bull* (Amherst, NY: Prometheus, 2004).

G. L. Hardcastle and G. A. Reisch, *Bullshit and Philosophy* (Peru, IL: Open Court, 2006).

CHAPTER 2

1. It's what I received from my then-12 year-old son who was hitting me up for a cell phone when I asked "How come you need one?" His response, "Because then you can always reach me." I responded with a sarcastic, "Sure."

2. What's missing is *covert* either because you can't figure out what it is or you know something is missing that almost everyone knows should be present but you aren't able to identify the purpose served by its absence.

3. V. Packard, *The Hidden Persuaders* (New York: David McKay, 1957).

4. Obvious others include excessive compliments, gratuitous favors, lip-service acknowledgment, subversively conducted politics, maintaining face, high-status possession showiness, guilt inducement, self-advancing charitable giving, dressing for success, staged appearances, literary license, withheld facts, cover-ups, kissing up, status symbols, physical affectations, body positioning, giving the silent "treatment," visible emoting, answering questions not asked, answers that fail to address key issues in the question asked, etc.

CHAPTER 3

1. Illustrated by Chapter 1's case in S. A. Culbert and J. J. McDonough, *The Invisible War: The Pursuit of Self-Interests at Work* (New York: Wiley, 1980).

2. Frankfurt, *On Bullshit*.

CHAPTER 5

1. An estimate of the modified point of aim required to compensate for wind or for target movement when firing a rifle.

CHAPTER 6

1. Quotes are excerpted from a story by Bill Sing, "Fed Chief Learns His Microphone Is Never Off," in *Los Angeles Times*, May 24, 2006, p. C1.

CHAPTER 7

1. Culbert and McDonough, *Radical Management*.

2. Culbert, *Mind-Set Management*.

CHAPTER 8

1. Coalition Provisional Authority Head Paul Bremmer, Secretary of State Donald Rumsfeld, and CIA Director George Tenet were awarded Medals of Freedom and three-star General Ricardo Sanchez was nominated for a fourth star. That nomination was withdrawn only after it was realized that the Senate Armed Services Committee would not confirm him.

2. Culbert, *Mind-Set Management*; see Chapter 16.

3. What's more, often the initial compensation figure was derived as a fraction of a departmentwide budget with any subsequent enhancement having trickle-around effects. The department has now exceeded their budgetary allocation. Does that mean someone who was given more is now going to have some of their promised enhancement cut back?

4. I realize what I'm advocating, in the name of "realism," contrasts with the belief that merit should be rewarded. Any boss thinking that way is free to give pay enhancements to superior performers. But doing so does not imply that you can look at someone's paycheck and accurately form conclusions about the "objective" value of performance received. There will always be instances of "lower results" performers receiving a bigger check than people whose contributions the boss values more.

5. Culbert and Ullmen, *Don't Kill the Bosses!*

CHAPTER 9

1. See Culbert and McDonough, *The Invisible War.*

CHAPTER 10

1. G. Vickers, *Freedom in a Rocking Boat* (New York: Basic Books, 1971).

2. S. A. Culbert, *The Interpersonal Process of Self-Disclosure: It Takes Two to See One* (Washington, DC: NTL Institute, 1967).

CHAPTER 11

1. S. A. Culbert, *The Organization Trap* (New York: Basic Books, 1974).

CHAPTER 12

1. *Meet the Press*, July 30, 2006.

2. This term was coined by Carl Rogers and conceptualized in his book *On Becoming A Person* (New York: Houghton Mifflin, 1961).

3. R. Benedict, *The Chrysanthemum and the Sword* (New York: Houghton Mifflin, 1974).

APPENDIX A

1. Reformulated from that appearing in Culbert, *Mind-Set Management*.

INDEX